delicate
strange

Poems and Stories
by
Jessica Ruby Radcliffe

HIGH BOHEMIA
NEW ORLEANS, LOUISIANA USA

Photo on page 136 by
©Katie Veltum Cartwright

ISBN: 978-0692508602

United States • United Kingdom • Europe • Australia • India

The bed is the altar of the night
the table is the altar of the day
we ourselves are the offering.

CONTENTS

MY VOICE

My voice is the wind through bare branches
it is a well worn path
snow falling in pale light
and footsteps on dry leaves

my voice is an owl
and the shadow of an owl in flight
my voice is the startled eye of a rabbit
and the smell of crushed pine needles

my voice is a prayer book
and a dictionary
and a small stained cook book
it is a poem murmured ceaselessly into the ear of an old soldier
a cricket in the corner
whiskey in a glass

the first few drops of rain
the last few miles of a journey
the wind in bare branches
and the footsteps of a loved one
safely returned at a late hour

my voice
is the door closing gently
softly
warm in the cold night
and outside
the wind
and the creak of bare branches

THE WIND IS UP
Hurricane Isaac

The wind is up.

From the other side of St Claude
a rooster crows over and over
announcing the hurricane
I am watching out the front door
Skinny Feral Kitty
looks up at me from the street
with eyes not quite as bold.

Day 1.

Aug 28 spent waiting for a hurricane, early tears freak out... take ashwaghanda herb, relax. Inside kitty, Lady Pru sits in the bedroom window, lace curtains billowing around her. Outside cat Archie jumps out the window, intent on exploration.

The wind is up.

The builders next door have not dealt with their rubbish, and by tomorrow it could be everywhere; not shattering my windows, I pray. Everything from my yard is now in the shed, battening all the hatches. With everything outside put away, and the bathtub filled with emergency water, there is nothing more to do but wait.

I spent the next three hours playing dress up with jewelry and make up, was going to wear a ball gown but decided to begin a painting and didn't want to get paint on my gown; so, dark eyed and heavily bejeweled, I painted and listened to weather news all day, with facebook time and a few worried out of town phone calls.

Doc Otis drove over mid afternoon in the high wind, and we talked as he watched me paint. After he left both cats came inside, and I was in bed by 8:30. Auntie Dawna called at 9 and I was half asleep. I said, "whatever happens, don't believe the news on tv. They are evil. We are fine." She said, "ok, then go back to sleep."

Day 2

How do cats know when it's 6 am? Archie is hiding a little pocket watch. There is no electricity, no phone, I am up with a flashlight to feed the cats. Is there running water? yes! gas stove? yes!

I try using this time to make modeling clay doll parts but it's horribly humid, with no fan and no air conditioning, they may not dry before they disintegrate.

Since there is no electricity, any food in the fridge has to be used quickly or it will go bad. For breakfast I made soup out of leftover spaghetti sauce, odd bits of cheese, and an open pint of soymilk, seasoned further with umeboshi plum vinegar and mineral bouillon. Cream of tomato soup, lovely. I worked on the painting all morning. The phone is still charged and it buzzes with a tornado watch warning. The wind howls and speaks like a man. Leaves and twigs blow by the window in front of the house - like Dorothy in the Wizard of Oz, flying through the air wild spinning in circles. More makeup. I slept in my jewelry and it's much too hot for a ball gown, or any gown. The bathroom ceiling is not leaking, maybe because it is a misty wild rain, not buckets from heaven rain. It's a good day for runes and tarot cards, for divination, when there is no civilized electricity messing with the etheric realms.

At 1 pm Kathleen texts from the Lower 9th Ward to say she wishes she had more ice. I answered that I was lonely but I have everything I need. That will be the final text of the week.

Naptime, almost asleep BIG noise CRACK explodes through the cacophony of wind outside.

Sounds like a transformer exploded or something, suddenly rocking the sound waves mighty, pure wild quick and LOUD. Later see that it had been the sound of a myrtle tree across the street, broken off by its roots, out of the earth.

Day 3

The following morning, in the dark kitchen, no electricity, I make 3 bean soup — coffee, cocoa and soymilk...heat slowly, add sugar but not too much. Perfect.

Lady Pru sits on my chest and belly in the stormy morning with gentle insistent head butts. She has been biting. Archie is already out of his mind on catnip, sprawled across the kitchen table. It's dark in the back of the house...he lifts a louche Archie-paw as I pass..."meow."

Of course, he dreams of a world where he is a feline Oscar Wilde draped across the bed at Otter's house, and all his chores are done and there are no longer any dogs. Dream, Archie. High John the Conquerer.

With the windows open all day, I started two paintings. Archie slept all day on the catnip.

Pru with me constantly stepping in things and sleeping up against the painting. Next door they are having a party with food and drink. The National Guard was parked at St Claude and Congress "guarding the pharmacy", it has been said. Curfew is now at 8pm.

Very early this morning out the front window I saw a man wearing what appeared to be nothing but a yellow rain coat, no clothes or shoes or anything else. He passed the house and a few moments later came hurrying back the other way, the National Guard must have sent him home. Now it's 7pm, the light is fading in the house, weather not bad, must be the eye of the hurricane. It's very hot and humid and Lady Pru sits on the table beside me by the window to the street. I have vodka and cranberry juice "no ice" for dinner, then off to bed. I found a little book light, better than a flashlight for reading in bed. Tomorrow I'll be going out and about. Forty eight hours in the house is enough.

Sura just called from Los Angeles, so nice to hear from her. She will find out what's going on here and call me or text. Good. Katie also...uh oh, and now not able to text either... ah well, tomorrow is another day.

It's dark...I write by Herbie's big yellow flashlight. Sura called from the salon and gave me an update on news here. With no electricity there is no tv, no radio, and the internet is down anyway.

I am eating leftover rice and vegetables from the fridge. The cats are sleeping, the wind is up, door and windows open, rain spray wet but lovely.

The wind is noisy. Soon to bed but first a shower with my feet in the tub
of cold water saved for in case the water goes out.

nice

dark

rain

Sura text.

Find Judah, he's at Burning Man.

Cats and me in bed, bedroom window. Goodnight, rain.

    8:30 is the 11:00 of no electricity.

***

Day 4

Morning coffee, and all is still outside.

Earlier, at 6am "cats know" very dark and so very quiet, no rain, little
wind, cooler.

Herbie's big feather had blown off the wall, fallen to the tabletop in the
kitchen.

Outside a car alarm went off at about 7, a man across the street gave it
the Eye and it stopped. I watched him do this.

By 7:30 it was getting dark again, and the temperature dropped — storm
coming.

Just before this hurricane my friend Neti called me "solitary", like that's
okay and my choice. I am not "solitary", I am isolated, incredibly hurt,
and frightened. I am also brave and often peaceful. I long for company.
Intelligent, warm, quiet, kind. Ah, sirens...civil society's return.

It's still cool and dark, raining tropical big sloppy drops. I am perfumed
and kohled, wearing pearls and gold, and have incensed the temple completely,
blessed the cat, other cat has gone out, blessed in absentia, coffee made,
now to paint.

I am Schmata Minx, three days alone in the temple, painting a spiral snake
on a round table top, and a large portrait of the Norse goddess Freya.

Went out!

I walked down the street and borrowed an egg from Denise and Marshall, took them an Abita, which they didn't really need, being fully stocked. I wanted to bake something, then remembered the oven is electric, the stove burners are gas, electricity has been off for days. Our curfew is now from 8pm to 6am. Tomato rice soup for breakfast, snake painting is almost done, food in the fridge is still cold enough, but the freezer is beginning to defrost. Mostly soup and mac n cheese in there.

Dreamt of Herbie. He said "yes" and let go of my hand, then I woke up.

It's getting pretty nice out. I have been by the window in the front room every day. Lady Pru is mostly on the table helping me paint or looking outside at the weather. I like drawing light, and stars. It feels so magical; they just come out of the darkness alive.

Doc Otis stopped by in his car and took me to Rouses to get ice for me and his friend Ember.

First we tried Mardi Gras Zone which had lots of Bywater types milling around and no power, then to Café Flora which was also dark though open and Ali was playing chess with someone inside. He looked very tired.

Next, off to Mary's Ace Hardware on Rampart — still no radio for me and no batteries for Otis but lots of other stuff. At Walgreen's in the French Quarter we got his batteries and good advice about ice from the cashier — the ice depot on Decatur and Marigny, I didn't even know it existed.

First we went to Rouses in the CBD. It had a generator and was buzzing like a town square with deli food, groceries, air conditioning, coffee, wireless, little tables. Otis paid for my groceries, about $40, which was very nice of him. We went back into the Marigny to get ice and then he took me to my house in the Bywater and went to check on Ember, who lives in my old apartment near the racetrack. Aurelia came by this morning and took pictures of the tree that fell across the street. She is sweet to check on me. There's no phone or tv or radio, we have no idea what's going on out there. I heard the radio in Otis's car, apparently some places are badly flooded, but not New Orleans.

Cooked, swept out leaf debris that had blown in, went for a walk. Visited Mark Bingham in the gloom of unlighted Piety Street Studio, where he was cooking unfrozen dumplings from the Hong Kong Market. He poured me

14

a cognac and served me a dumpling. Very civilised. Back home ate my own dinner and sealed the snake painting. Marshall and Denise were out walking Stitch and came by with 3 more eggs. Love. They have a generator and took my phone home with them to charge it.

The humidity is rising. I am strangely covered with little bruises. The Saints play an away game tonight, seems unreal, very few tvs, maybe some at bars with generators running, or in the French Quarter.

I panicked today at the Rouses, ok home alone, lonely but ok. Got some lovely curly dancing branches from the downed tree, also a penny that had grown into its deep roots and was freed by the storm. I am tired, stressed out and feel slightly ill, and I hope the electricity comes back on before the temperature rises.

At 8 pm, dogs bark, and out on the street a bicycle stops. It's so quiet outside in this big city I can hear the bicycle's brakes from in here.
Bed time is darktime...I know there is some worry about West Nile virus, because it's so hot and all the windows are open, but mosquitos are probably still recovering from the storm so they shouldn't be a problem for a few nights yet. And maybe we will be electrified any minute now.

The moon has been eclipsed
only once have I ever seen the moon
there is no other time
fitful night
one strange nightmare

Day 5

Pru woke me up at 3 am to let Archie in the front door, like a good sister and then I slept til 8 am! Archie had hopped back out an open window and Pru did not wake me at 6.

I have been studying Freya for her portrait. Humid and hot today, so said the car radio yesterday. The hurricane painting is finished, a giant cosmic snake in space, and it's not too hot so far, maybe 85 degrees with a slight breeze. My heart is troubled, tears are close, thinking of love and living and what to do. Someone is driving around like crazy up and down St Claude for the past hour. The sounds of chainsaws and hammers are in the air everywhere, people are biking and walking past, and the bicycle tour even came by this morning.

food stamp office 8885243576 cant get them
no electricity no phone landline no refrigerator
no radio no computer or tv no air conditioning
local bank and pharmacy closed, St Anna's church dark and closed.

• §≈§≈§≈§≈§≈§≈§≈§≈§≈§ •

Day 6

Three am full moon moonlight bright as daylight shines in the bedroom window which is wide open, curtains pulled aside for any air. It is cooler, about 75, with a very light rain. Archie is outside, Pru goes from the foot of the bed to the windowsill to lying on my chest and purring loudly. I think the people next door may be sleeping in their car with the engine running and the a/c on...or maybe they decided to end it all. I must find a way to use internet today...I think this is Saturday. It is said that 84% of New Orleans has no electricity, and we did not evacuate - no evacuation order was given in fact. How many days has it been?

It's all fine until we run out of food, and money for booze and cigarettes.
My freezer is almost melted, must share this food [or throw it away], and then the closest food is miles away unless Wagner's Liquor and Meat has food...must check later. Ice is in the Marigny.
I hope the fridge stays healthy. I will need money soon, Judah said he would send money after Burning Man.
I guess Sura would help me if I asked. I wish I didn't have to ask.
Barb Metz sent $20, I will send her a parking fairy or something later. Kyla and Oliver sent $50, which paid for cat flea meds, so glad about that. Anne Marie owed $60 which paid for the second half of the phone bill. Christina ordered 3 dolls, I made them, that's $75 but had not been paid yet and she's probably left town now. There may be $50 in the bank, closed due to storm, can check online. Amzie said internet is available at Rouses, or Cafe Envie. He will always give me money if it's an emergency.

In the morning I will walk to Envie, it's closest. If there is more money maybe buy a cooler, or no just use the freezer with a block of ice in a garbage bag? A big cooler would be really useful...and a battery powered radio.

I don't have ANY money.

5:45 am dreamed Sally Anne Glassman kissed me as we flew around the room together. CAW CAW CAW outside thrummm thrumm thrummm from the river and just after dream waking large spider bite on right groin.

Cats are up, I fed them, and fed skinny feral kitty [outside], hope his cousins don't find out.
Fed him out front last night and skinny black kitty came over, but I'm pretty sure she has a home.
Archie guarded skinny feral kitty so he could eat his kibbles in the planter box next door.
I am up at dawn with the cats for all the daylight hours we can muster. It is still dark in the kitchen, and there is fierce cawing from the street. Archie has returned from his nightly perambulations, skinny feral kitty is under the house being terrorised by a big orange tom.

It was cooler last night
lying naked in the moonlight with my hair down
wearing the hurricane ring
no covers needed all night but not too hot either
no mosquitos.

This is what really happened yesterday:
I put on some clothes and packed up computer, cell phone, all chargers, put the bag in the rolling wire shopping basket, rolled it down to the bus stop on St Claude in the Bywater and within 10 minutes the 88 was there [you really never know, it could have taken hours], took the bus to Esplanade, got off and walked toward the river towards Cafe Envie. Amzie told me the day before that people were getting online from there. On the way I saw Jack, an old friend of Coco's and Mr. Earl; I only know him from hanging out at Mr. Earls on Royal Street a long time ago, when Kabuki was next door and Rania and I lived on Esplanade, and Amzie was my darling. Jack said people had been getting online in his building and I was welcome

to come up, so I did. I have always wanted to see where Jack lives. It is gorgeous, perfect but had no internet so I drank a cup of cold coffee and left right away.

Café Envie was not crowded but no one could get online there either. The password was Matt Dillon.

People were lovely, sharing space and information, and I had another actually very good cup of coffee and was about to pack up and leave when I saw Arturo. We talked for a while about the inner working of the outer ways, and I gave him a hug. Then off to find ice, the plan was to walk it in the rolling cart back home to the Bywater. I was beginning to feel panicky, it was supposed to be find a way to read email and clean out the fridge day, and I had to have ice or risk losing the rest of the food.

I walked to the ice depot across from 511 Marigny; it was early but they were already very busy and sadly when I got to the head of the line it seemed that all the cheap ice was gone and there were only $6 bags left. They could only take cash because the computer was down and I only had $4 so walked away iceless, trying not to dissolve in tears, having been very stoic so far. If only I hadn't bought that cup of coffee... I looked around for someone to ask for $2, maybe a workman or someone with outside connections, then saw Don from St Anna's Church. He greeted me with a hug and asked how everything was going and of course I finally melted into tears and told him I needed $2 for ice and he said 'this won't do, wait right here' so I stood on the hot steamy sidewalk in front of the Friendly Bar with my rolling basket full of no internet and no ice and Don came back with a roll of 20's, bottles of cold water and a bag of canned food. He then walked down the block to the ice depot, bought a large bag, came back, loaded me and the basket and the ice and the food into his air conditioned car and directed his partner Rusty to drive me home, please.

Thank you thank you thank you, no more tears.

I tore into the fridge, throwing away thawed old bread ends and ancient soup. As that job was concluding I heard Otis yelling at the front door. He had his car and would take me anywhere because he was bored and hungover, so we went to Rouses again to try to get online there. It was like a jumping little village, and one woman with beautiful dia de los muertos tattoos said she'd been there for 3 days. We both got online at one of the little tables in the deli, and saw a map of power outages [80% of the city] bought supplies [money thanks to Don and Rusty] including a large bottle of vodka which can be important fuel for some of us in navigating cataclysmic aftermath. Kept trying to find a battery powered radio but still no luck though Walmart on Tchoupitoulas was open. Stopped at the ice depot to get ice for Otis, because I already had some, and he took me home. We ate mac n cheese from my freezer and I gave him two containers of slightly unfrozen vegetable soup for later. Then he went home to deal with his own fridge. A fridge ignored can go seriously bad as we all know, after Katrina.

Kathleen and Ben have been partying on their deck and I have not gone, due to no car no phone and no one came to get me...maybe tonight will find a ride...take 88 the other way and walk? A New Orleans truth: crazy old white ladies can go almost anywhere. Just look hoodoo.

Spent the rest of the daylight hours painting. Hot and stuffy, moving slow, white wine and ice.

At dusk went out in the backyard for the first time since the storm. Swept and cleared large branches by throwing them back over the fence to the yard where the tree is growing. Put the empty planters back up, it's too hot and humid to grow anything at this time of year so they are all empty but put them back up in the shade anyway. Took a cold shower and was in bed by 8:30 dark and sleepy

long day
tired clean naked
moonlight sleep

Day 6

Cooler morning air napping in so tired and have been so hot, it's exhausting. All so quiet except for crows, still and dreaming at 7 am, perhaps it will rain today?

By noon had finished cleaning up the yard and put mulch down. Neti came by in her car, bringing a cooler, ice, wonderful fruit and vegetables. I only realized how worn out I was feeling when, lying on the bed nearly naked with a large bag of ice on my stomach, it was still too hot to breathe and I actually snapped at Neti, my savior. Yikes.

Gina's sprinkler party in the Holy Cross!

19

We hopped into Neti's car taking all my extra freezer food to the Lower 9 where Ben and Kathleen and Rosemary and a lot of other people were sitting around a large sprinkler/mister in various types of dilapidated yard furniture, drinking heavily and telling stories. We ate the last of everything from everyone's now thawed freezers and cooled off, getting very wet at the same time. At dusk Gina drove me back over the bridge in her truck, and just as we got to my house in the Bywater - ELECTRICITY!

Those of us who live in New Orleans know that the real meaning of a hurricane can only be measured alone in the dark, or in a group when you would do anything you could to help but there's so little you can do. We make each other laugh, we let each other cry, we are very still at our center and wild on the outside, like the storm. And as Hurricane Isaac reminded us, it's never really over.

MINERVA

I am tired
and my wings are so heavy
I hear ghost-dogs in the night
gnawing on cracking bones
a dream foretells the year of my death
my guardian angel pulls closer

ancient of days
the owl of Minerva flies at dusk
in a quiet glory of feathers

hidden in the underbrush of longing
my wild heart
the high pitch of heart break
calls its own fate

I have not been tamed
I am wiser than before
I know more about the hand that feeds me
I am tired
but I have not been tamed

I Came Here From New Orleans

I came here from New Orleans
I have perfume and petticoats
pretty things from my grandmothers
etched glassware, feathers and striped stockings
two Erzulie veves and
a black cat bone.
That was home,
tattooed market princesses
pretty boys and hard cases
too many piano players
and all the wrong boyfriends.
One little girl said
"I want my weddin' to be just like
one of y'all's funerals"...
Yes
hand me down my big boots
and my bright red and my purple
and my blue lace
say goodbye to the Mississippi
hot swampy nights
breezes and beer on the levee
catfish heads and bullet casings
flood waters comin up holy
art, magic, betrayal,
mystery
humidity and stupidity
and always the water
comin up holy
comin up holy
  antique glass beads and gold earrings
  vodka and iced tea
"that's how we live when we're ruined" said she

kiss me
oh
kiss me hard
as we pass the graveyard.

CINDERELLA
Hurricane Katrina

Pluto, the god of the underworld
was amused at being called 'dead, as a planet'
"of course I'm dead! I'm the GOD of the Dead!"
***
Cinderella
dressed in yellow
went upstairs to kiss a fellow
made a mistake
kissed a snake
how many doctors did it take?
***
why are our bones so white?
I washed the blood out of my hair
why is our blood so red?
I washed and washed
to wash off the rancid stink of him
and our tears? our tears are salt
salt in the wound
two stitches closed one wound...
how did my mother raise such a FOOL?
***
I see construction workers and I see
blood on the street, where there is no blood.
And I feel threat, where there is no threat
because it's in me...only the fear in me
right? is that right?
***
We are rebuilding New Orleans.
a few weeks ago
my friend got his throat slit
French Quarter, nelly deli
middle of the night...
there was blood on the sidewalk, I saw it

and I saw him in the hospital bed
like a big bad angel baby
tatts and rings, tubes and bandages
Dr Frankenstein stapled him back together
he said the only thing he was afraid of was the doctor
***
we been blown away
like a dandelion seed
blown off far from the mother weed.
my mother said
if you're going through hell-
keep going
***
I lost my glasses
I'm living on bluff
walking a thin thin line
can't find stuff
living in a camper on Mandeville St
New Orleans
first spring days after
the end of the world
***
Around the corner, where Bucky hung himself
and Helen was shot
behind a ragged screen door
a smoker is coughing
yeah, I know that sound
somebody else is dying of their wounds
***
When I die, take pictures of my tattoos
for the grandchildren
take a lock of hair
take an embrace for the lover I never held
take some grace
and take a good look at my face
tell my grandchildren
"I have been dreaming of you my whole life
just as our ancestors dream of me...

perhaps what we are is the sum total of
the dreams of millions , distilled
who come before us.
We embrace, and add our dreams to the mix
and then one day, beloved, you are born
use it well and dream kindly..."

tell them that nothing is profane
everything is sacred
tell them the street is our altar
and we are the offering
purity is an innate quality of existence
say, "this is the only power:
there is a compass in your heart
tell the truth
then when you speak,
what you say will be true."
***
In the house of the soul
all the sorrows come at once
that is, they all live in the same
hall of the heart
sorrow upon sorrow, they inform each other
and every leavetaking resounds
in the leavetaking chamber of the heart
and every joy lives at once
all the joy resounds in the same
joyous temple of the heart
the sorrow and the joy
resounding always throughout
the house of the soul

open doors, closed doors...

I am in the kitchen of the house of the soul
crying in the soup
I am in the kitchen
and tears are the broth of this soup

I sing a little song
while I am chopping vegetables

I sing a song of birth and death
of joy and heartbreak
of longing and fulfilment
longing   fulfilment
longing, oh longing
and, fulfilment
this is the lesson of the ocean waves
there will always be another longing
and there will always be another fulfilment
this is the lesson of lovemaking
always another longing
always another fulfilment
hastening towards
putting off the moment of
that little death
***
An Englishman thinks 100 miles is a long way
an American thinks 100 years is a long time
I think as deeply as I dare
and then thought stops
thought cannot cross the yellow tape barrier
of the heart
and beyond that magical border there is
only knowing, and there I wander
caught in a web of wondering...

New Orleans appears to be situated very near
a tear in the fabric of reality
the Sufis say
"the king is in rags, the castle in ruins"...
and what becomes of the old full moon?
my darlings, it crumbles into pieces
and becomes the stars

my cup is half full

I rail against the emptiness
as I splash about in the half-fullness

***

WHERE YOU GONNA RUN TO
WHEN THE WORLD'S ON FIRE
WHERE YOU GONNA RUN TO
WHEN THE WORLD'S ON FIRE
WHERE YOU GONNA RUN TO
WHEN THE WORLD'S ON FIRE
LITTLE DARLING
WHEN THE WORLD'S ON FIRE?

***

It was so quiet after the fire
charcoal has a different resonance
than wood and plaster...
the wind off the Mississippi
is cool in the early morning.
I sit with my back to the rising sun
my dog is lying in the sand
underneath the camper.
The petunias need water
this winters pansies cough out
a few more straggly blossoms.
It is April in New Orleans

sweeping my house in the dark
I looked in the dirt
and found a strand of tiny pearls...
I dusted them off on my apron and
hung them on a hook by the door
this is how it is in my little camper home
laundry spread like Tibetan prayer flags
drying in the sun...

Time has stood still here
people have become more real
focus sharper
Nature has moved to her rightful place

at the head of the banquet table
all hail the moment
all hail each other
 all we have is the moment
all we have is each other
***
GONNA USE YOUR BOSOM FOR MY PILLOW
GONNA USE YOUR BOSOM FOR MY PILLOW
GONNA USE YOUR BOSOM FOR MY PILLOW
LITTLE DARLING
WHEN THE WORLD'S ON FIRE
***
Don't tell Katrina stories
tell Katrina truths
I came home in October and my
house was still there

pain was everywhere/on every wall
many people had taken refuge
back then I still had a bed
many people had slept in my bed
there were candles everywhere
and under the bed
a stash of crumpled Bible verses
and in the kitchen, looted groceries,
like seven cans of Walgreens chocolate
covered peanuts
two full bottles of Zoloft
five hammers
bee pollen from upstate New York
three drums, a guitar, and a saxaphone.

but where is my dog?

does absence really make the heart
grow fonder?
will you love me most
if you never see me again?

Kabir says
"have pity on me, oh ye my friends
for the hand of God has touched me"
I want to wear white, and cry
I want to pick flowers
that only last for one day
pick them in their delicate profusion
and then
pick them again tomorrow.

FEELING HEART DOG

weep carefully, my friends
if your tears are too bitter
they will eat away at your heart's eyes
and you will never see clearly again

Due to having lived an early life filled with crushing responsibility,
betrayal, poverty and psychedelics, I have washed up on the shores of the
Mississippi with a medical condition known as clinical depression, in touch
with a sorrow which feels at times almost too great to bear. This means
that I must carefully monitor the bitterness level of my tears. If my tears
become too bitter they may eat away at my heart's eyes, and I might never
see clearly again. To aid in this endeavor, the Center for Universal Healing
has issued me with a Feeling Heart Dog. My Feeling Heart Dog has been
trained by the angels at The Center for Universal Healing to get me out
of bed in the morning, to make sure I go outside for at least 15 minutes
every day even if it's raining, that I walk, and meet other people, many of
who may actually suffer from a similar complaint and are accompanied by
their own Feeling Heart Dogs. She makes sure that I own at the very least
a can opener and a bowl, that I know how to find fresh water, that I don't
wander off with a stranger, and that each day closely resembles the last in
a fairly healthy way.

A Feeling Heart Dog
means never alone at night
never out drinking for more than a few hours
Dogs don't get bitterness or irony
so, if my complaints are ignored
I know they need to be reframed quickly
sweetened.
And yet, I have to walk, frightened and alone in the dark
to read these poems to you
because Seeing Eye Dogs and Hearing Ear Dogs can go to bars
but Feeling Heart Dogs are not allowed.
They are also not allowed on the streetcar,

which makes it almost a poetic experience
getting out of the neighborhood and back .
Walking home through the French Quarter
unleashed and panic stricken
my heart is filled with bitter tears
I attempt to sweeten them with vodka
carefully, carefully
will you take me home?
where is my dog?

• §≈§≈§≈§≈§≈§≈§≈§≈§≈§≈§ •

post script...in the years since this piece was written, Feeling Heart Dogs
have gained acceptance in the medical community.

FOR DR. MARTINIÉ

when I walk out with Lu
we might be invisible
we walk a thin line
we are called
then and never
ancient and tomorrow
walking NOW
each step on the razors edge of truth

faded black
threadbare
long and thin
gentle wisdom from cruel stars
Lu picks a most delicate path
calm
through the burning places
through the drowning places
through the buried places

at his side
I am a fine wild human
djinn and angel
dakini bound
and putting feathers on his edges
rich colors
ribbons flying
snapping in the wind
above his skittish gentility

we walk our own time hidden path
we may be invisible
but we know where we are going
and that place is invisible too
ratty tat tat

leaning into the soft air of New Orleans
vision clear in the always half light
questing
we share that state
where nothing is ever finished
and everything is asleep
except the two of us
walking dreamers
blessings in disguise
between the worlds
and everywhere
alive

SOUTHERN DECADENCE

Soft early morning light,
heartbreak in the air,
sweet fragile longing
and a sense of obstinate misrule...
there's no place like home.
Bless you boys,
mourn your dead.
Dress, fuck, and over drink
pluck your lucky stars out of the sky
and wear them for the weekend.

A Lot of Things Can Happen in the Course of Forever

This love is not like wine
or some rare cognac
it is more of a fine balsamic vinegar
which, if used sparingly
makes everything heavenly
but no one would want it by the glass
perhaps unfortunately
his glass is half full of this vinegar
and mine is half empty

perhaps it's all just a game
and eventually
I will be too old to play
and eventually
you will be too old
when the little girls ring your bell
you will say
'quiet, child, I was sleeping'
and they will long for your
beautiful old body
then you will slip deliciously
into half-dreams
searching for memories of me

NEW ORLEANS NOV 2005

Evening in the Fauberg Marigny
it's raining and
there's no electricity
I am alone and I stink
that wild high woman-smell of garlic
and a brief encounter with the arts
a brief encounter with the artist
formerly known as impossible
now known only as unlikely

there has been no hot water since early September
a few days into the flood
a few days after the hurricane
now things come and go
the electricity has gone off again
wfaded blue velvet drapes
open to the warm wet velvet night
rain patters gently beyond torn lace curtains

I was asleep when this rain began
and barely waking
I imagined it was
the artist
in the kitchen
with a fork
gently patting tuna and mayonnaise
on slices of raisin bread...
pat pat pat   pat pat pat

but no, he's gone
it's the rain
I am alone in my bed in the dark
it's November
I really need a shower
there's no hot water
and it's raining.

I Wanted To Call You
July 2008

I wanted to call you and say
"isn't this an amazing rainstorm"
but then I realized we were really thousands of miles apart
and now we will have different rainstorms.

Our first goodbye was in New Mexico
We had barely said hello,
I was 18, and I wanted you;
you danced away from me in the dust,
perhaps forever.
Our next goodbye was a hundred years later,
at a small hotel on Chartres Street
you let me bathe you
hot water on a hot night
in the big Victorian tub
I washed your beard with my hands
we made love in clean white sheets...
you gave me the little silver potion pot
shaped like a horn
and capped with a dark blue eye
I gave you a tiny gold ring
with a pale blue eye
and I would be Gala
and you would be Salvador
though only by a trick of time
because surely
they would have been us
had we lived before them
you took my picture in the mirror
and left me there before the night was up,
and I was off to England

The next time we said goodbye

was on the bed in your studio
and we laughed
and you took my picture in the tiger hat
among the canvases and paint pots
fancy clothes and music
mirrors and old photographs, mayonnaise jars and computer parts
Horse Badorties
I lay on your shoulder
where you smell like pot and coffee
even though you don't smoke pot,
it is a mystery of life-
like the saints in India
who spontaneously put forth attar of roses
but you smelled of pot and coffee
and me.
[in the days before the red musk oil]
I am not jealous anymore
I still long for you sometimes
I long for what you are not
and I love you anyway.

The last time we said goodbye
I didn't know it was goodbye
I thought it was hello...
someday we may say goodbye again,
but this time
you're really gonna miss me.

I'm Wondering If Jesus Had a Girlfriend

Church doctrine tells us
[perhaps by omission]
that Jesus slept with no woman
he played no musical instrument
he didn't write poetry
or paint
or howl at the moon

Tom Robbins suggests that
Christianity, as we know it,
is the perfect wedge
a system
for turning priestesses into handmaidens
queens into concubines
and goddesses into muses...
and can you imagine what has become
of the nymphs?

but maybe he wasn't really like that

I'm wondering if Jesus had a girlfriend
did he hold her face so gently
in his rough hands
did he sometimes smooth long dark hair
away from her desert dry cheek
and nibble gold earrings
did he care so very much
what she thought and felt
did he come to her for healing
and balance and words of wisdom
did she give him
loaves and fishes
and green herbs and salt and olive oil

did she say
"how much water would you like in your wine?"
and
"forty days and forty nights in the desert
might do you a lot of good"
and
"somehow I just don't trust that one apostle..."

did she kiss him deep
and pull his hair
did he love the spicy warm smell of her
her shape
the way she moved
her hand resting on his arm

did she bring him joy?
did he bring her bracelets from Jerusalem?

did the thought of her heartbreak
break his heart
did she nearly die when he did
did they adore each other?

I'm wondering if Jesus had a girlfriend

HUNGRY FOR EVERYTHING
Christmas Eve 2006 / 511 Marigny

Hungry for everything
I am living on faith and starlight...
living in New Orleans
is like riding an alligator
and for sure nobody's going to mess with you
except maybe the alligator

During the second December after Hurricane Katrina, in dismal winter drizzle, I was living alone in a camper on the burnt out site where my house once stood. I was badly injured in April and I ran away, to California and back, spending months in a spun out frightened daze. My own dog Rania was still in California, where she would die before we met again.

Hungry for food, water, hope, warmth and companionship, I agreed to keep an eye on a friend's dog over the week of Christmas. My friend lived in a big drafty studio room, where he had electricity but no running water, in a building full of other writers and artists. It was a lot like camping only safer and a bit dryer. On Christmas Eve there would be lots to drink but no food, with people coming and going throughout the evening.

The dog and I walked out into a cold damp wind, to the only food store left in our corner of New Orleans. There I bought a little chicken, frozen solid; an onion, a few potatoes, and a cabbage. Thawing the chicken in a cold building with only a hotplate ended up taking hours of boiling. I was determined to make this food before everyone got too drunk and obnoxious to eat, myself included.

It was a close call. Culinary note to self: never thaw a whole chicken by boiling, as this is not ideal.

Merry Christmas...a tough but tasty boiled dinner, all over but the shouting by 10 pm.

After eating, me and the big dog went back to our own cold quiet room. The atmosphere was wildly unsettled and heartbroken, creative and confused. Scattering gold and silver glitter stars all over the floor, lighting a dressed candle and saying every prayer I could; for me, and the building, and the dogs and all the sick fucks who were my friends and whirled around terribly damaged New Orleans in a mutated probably lucky to be alive end of the year mess, I rolled well fed into warm covers in the bed, alone, and so to sleep.

Christmas Morning 2006

And in a dream early morning
I see that someone with a great love in her heart
blessed this building
she mixed her magic into the mortar a long time ago
it's all held together by that ancient breath
wind and water blown in through holes in walls and windows
still it stands
the blessing has held firm
the building crumbling
held together with spirit
mysteriously blessed with a blessing that sings
between the bricks

waking to the sound of
the train so near
as it whistles through the city
its cry is
a shower of golden light in the dawn
and a ships horn answers from the foggy Mississippi
call and response
"we are here" and "we are here"

BEAUTIFUL DARKNESS

worship in the wind
a rumble of hosanna in the rock
liquid silver voices in the waves
the crackle of forever in the fire

brighter than my brightest remembering
holy days
whole nights
dark of the moon
inside / outside all the same
everything waits to take the next breath
death of before
birth of everafter

beautiful darkness when I am alone
beautiful darkness that carries me home
here in the darkness I'm always at home
beautiful beautiful darkness

VALENTINE'S DAY

a message between lovers
Chango to Yemaya

Here I am, in the late morning,
pacing the Bolinas sea wall
fiercely
the tide as high as it can be
the sky ribbons of piles of cloud
white and grey
on a grey day slightly wet not windy

and I have come offering
two little bullets
I picked up by the tracks
on Press Street at Burgundy
in New Orleans

I have held them for more than a year
awaiting the moment
trading them to Yemaya
Water Mother
for peace
an end to discord
in my heart

here at the sea wall
overlooking
breathing in
the great grey blue Pacific
I wear her colors
and send a prayer
a message

Chango sends you his love
this Valentines Day

here are these two bullets
metal heavy
from another water side
probably spat out of some child's gun
in a deadly midnight play fight

all the waters are the same waters
she reminds me
I know this and beloved Chango of the metal knows this
and oh La Pacifica wide and deep
sends her regards to the Mississippi Ma

and so I wait until I feel her smile
and she says yes, I accept this gift
and I feel the bullets
heavy in my small woman hand
I throw them
filled to the brim with discord
and she is happy to take them into her
where they will become Chango's children
dissolving back into metal in the depths of the sea

now I can go
and live the rest of my life
without the battles
and we have all done our work,
the gods and I
water, metal, little boys and men

later
she sends the moon with a message for me:
my heart is now a crescent boat
filled with light
set upon a calm dark sea
and
I am only responsible to love.

thank you

It's Spring

Shouting into doorways
come out come out you holy fools!
my heart is wild
the wheel has turned
it's spring!
what is the meaning of pride, or frustration?
look— a blossom!
leaf light and bird song!
the wheel has turned
with you or without you
come out come out you rowdy fucks
it sings its songs
and rings its bells
and couples because
one plus one equals three!
what joy!

and as I move toward that other light
and you move also
with each turn of the wheel
roll on bright sparks
spring will come
with us and without us
the wheel will turn
and every time I am amazed
because
one and one makes three
there is no beginning
and no end
let's pretend
it starts with
spring

I THOUGHT I SAW YOU IN A BOOK

I thought I saw you in a book
alive in grace and power
flesh and blood and bone
for her
I saw you in a book
and you looked back at me
do you remember?
flesh, blood, bone
head, heart, cock
hand and foot
her servant
strong and beautiful
alive in grace and power
dancing in the dark
was that not you?
dancing with the Moon?
I thought I saw you in a book
and you looked back at me
do you remember?

YOU TELL ME I'M BEAUTIFUL

Sometimes when you
tell me I'm beautiful, I go to the mirror and look
to see what it is you see
some hidden specialness
escaping momentarily
I want to know
what do I need to be
to be beautiful?
what is it about me
that is beautiful to you?
I want to capture it
distill it
nurture it
and give it to you in measured portions
when I'm feeling insecure
and then you will be
amazed and glowing
and pour your warmth on me
and you will tell me I'm beautiful
and I will know why
and that I can be beautiful again

Promise Me You Won't Be True

Promise me you won't be true
if I decide to sleep with you
and if I let you spend the night
as you already know I might
promise me with all your heart
and every single other part
promise me you won't be true
and I will do the same for you.

GLASS

The sound of civilization
the sound of glass
clinking against glass
milk bottles in the early morning
afternoon wind chimes
delicate and far away
in the evening
glass bracelets on both arms
perfume bottles on a mirrored table
I laugh as you look right through me
yes
to your health

Worshipping at the Altar of the Goddess of Extenuating Circumstances

for us, there is no tomorrow
tomorrow packed her bags
she's going with me
for all the good that's ever been
and all the good that is
I have laid down with men
who can't lie down
who seem to have no stillness in them
for too long I have been
worshipping at the altar of the
Goddess of Extenuating Circumstances
now she is Tara
now she is Kwan Yin
now she is co dependent
now she is a fucking idiot
it's like trying to tame a stray dog
so I can feed him
and teach him to howl at the moon
I want to say
it's your move, my friend
and there is no tomorrow
I say
don't put me on a pedestal
I'll bring you up there with me
and we'll both fall off
laughing and terribly hurt
tangled in each other
hands full of sky

SACRED WHOREHOUSE OF THE MOON

He said:
the wolf in me is howling
howling for the moon in you
I hear this howling
from my window
on the second floor of the
sacred whorehouse of the moon...
I am the daughter of Cleopatra and a monkey
soft eyes rimmed with kohl
curious envious unimpressed
peering out from behind a veil of gold curtains
all my sisters
all my sisters

listen:
he said
the wolf in me is howling
howling for the moon
in you

BEAUTIFUL ANDROID

What is age?
perhaps
spirit begins to show
through the cracks
in the mask of the
beautiful android
beautiful
and all around the edges
begins to glow
glowing in white hair
the light of the eternal
seeping out from around the closed door
of the body

TIME IS A LITTLE GIRL

Time is a little girl
who leans her lovely face
into yours
and smiles and takes your hand
and pulls you
laughing
through the back streets and boulevards
and in and out of windows
of not quite forever
and
someday
when she's tired of her play
she lets go of your hand

THE ALTAR OF THE NIGHT

I have dropped a treasure
in an unknown sea
I wait for you to dive
and bring it back to me
dreaming...
I kissed you by starlight
dreaming...
you said "yes" and let go of my hand

5 AM
when dreams beg for a place at the table
beg to be made real even for one day
they negotiate,
"please take me with you
make me real
I will be a tattoo
or a poem
I will be your lover until you really wake up...
is there only this 5 AM for us?" say the dreams
carefully, carefully
I search by heartlight and starlight
like luminous sonar
little boxes whisper faintly, "not here"
and then, "yes, perhaps, packed away in here".
sunlight and firelight and moonlight
are strong enough to hurt
I see by starlight and candlelight
 tree shade and mist
 heavy light deep and graceful
duende
dark light Kali
duende
sono clandestina
dreaming...

There is a thin line my darling
I know it all too well
I see you on a unicycle twenty feet up
on a wire
wavering...
we are very different
you are mad
I just have a broken heart
If you could localize your madness into a broken heart
you might find a way out, it says in this book,
a trip advisor,
"The Trip into Hades, to Bring Back a Box of Beauty".
Off I go,
wandering the city of love without a guidebook
sidestreets and alleyways
calling your name
searching my heart for the key to our little room
yesterday
for the moon
there was no sun

dreaming...
early still dark
it's only mid August but the days begin to grow shorter
cats up for cat breakfast
gentle thunder lightning cracks POW
rain and a little rain and more rain
I lie alone on the green couch where you tattooed my ankle
here
Saturday
sirens on the wind
and I wish you were holding me close
in the early storm coming morning
and it was raining
and the door open to the street.
These rooms are so empty
emptier than when you were here
and not with me

the call of the wild
and the call of the hearth
we are the moment between breaths
on a day out of time
down to the rind, the cob, the bone
take me now, take me home
the final quarter
of a life not lived to be described in prose.

You entered my room like Jacob wrestling with the Angel
you more righteous than eloquent
as obstinate as a forest violet
you in your hair shirt holding firmly to the wrong end of the stick
half idiot half angel
I say "this is your absolute last chance because I refuse to-"
you say "you're a classy broad for a gyppo"
beautiful mad delicate
your mind is made up
but your heart is an unmade bed
and if I come near I will definitely fall in ...
and after you'd gone I washed
I kissed the pillow where you'd laid
and wished you there
I wished your warmth around me
I cried for me and for you
and I slept like a wounded bird.
...
Dreaming
a task from Aphrodite to regain Eros the beloved:
Psyche must "descend into Hades, and retrieve a box of beauty"...
sleeping in the arms of benevolent mystery
we belong to the mossy earth
deep amber scented Goddess of night and dark and love
sleeping in forgiveness beauty hope
when I cry it's not only for myself
it's for you for us for everyone
who ever sought to unravel
the mad knot of love

Tell Your Father

when you see your father
tell him I love you
tell him I love you
and that we could have been safe together
safe and wild
tell him how you treasure me
and how you swore this was the best you could do
for me for you for him
for love for the art for poetry
for the whole world
tell him I love you and then
if he cares
maybe you can explain to him
why you sent me away
tell your father I love him for making you
and I always will
carry me gently in your heart
carry me like a summer queen
made of bees wing and spider web

ON MUSIC STREET

The wind is up,
 on Music Street
2:20 am
madly rattling doors and windows
3 am
mid November
the wind is wild
waking from a dream
of methodical detachment
create
love
let go
waking to the sudden fierce wind
on Music Street
as the black cat pounces trilling
on a grey mouse squeaking
a radio on in the back of the house
all the lights are on back there
the wind howls low
wild and dark on the street
next to my dark room
and the temperature is dropping
40 degrees overnight
as I wake sanguine
create love let go
even the train whistle sounds
matter of fact
and the insistent bell
at the crossing on St Claude
is only doing what it is paid to do
dark dark wind
empty
no shots no sirens no voices
and you

I know
somewhere not sleeping
and I here not asleep
as it becomes obvious
that a choice
a high holy choice a human conscious choice
a soul life
a life choice is swirling.
Use your sword to defend yourself
not against yourself
use your sword to defend yourself
brave soul.
Can you feel this wild wind from your tower?
big splashing raindrops
on my windows
the north wall of this house will leak
in the second window of the second room
and the side door.
Yohji is asleep in a pile of clothes
the mouse is gone
perhaps I will find it in the morning
wind chimes delicate
from their shelter on the front porch
on Music Street
I want you
I want you in bed with me
in the wild wind
and then warm in the cold morning.

November 2014
Feast of Hecate

OH MY DEAR

I love your beard
I love your hands
I will give you a silk shirt
and you can be barefoot
and shouting at shadows
and we will roll with the tides
I will dress you
and you will feel beautiful
and you will look at me and I will feel beautiful
and you will touch me and I will be beautiful
teaching each other the finer points
of things we don't know yet
jail house sailor cigarette rolling
and when to paint
and when to coffee
and how to shower with a woman who loves you
and kissing as a merciful art
art as everything
tie your hair back till it's white and only I
remember the auburn of your arms
you will have a silk shirt
coffee and cake
we will worship the thin line
push each other over
and gently
pull each other back
we will make a plan and break it a hundred times
and make a better one
and the weeks will pass like a hundred years
and the years like moments
and this stupid fucked up life won't be so fucked up after all.
I will paint the pain of your footsteps
the sorrow of your brushes
the sureness of your hands

the saving grace of your saving graces
I will paint inside me
and all I want is a kiss and to sleep with you

I SHOULD HAVE SAID

you said

what does it taste like?

and I should have said
stardust and roses
    hope
the Tibetan Book of the Dead
sprinkled with cocaine
and the spit of angels

I GAVE YOU WATER IN THE GRAIL CUP

When I gave you water in the grail cup
you gave me a strange look
I said
is it too good for you?
you said
nothing is too good for me
I took you at your word and I took you to bed
with deep electric velvet joy
and just a tiny touch of fear
Pandora's box opening
and it was almost dark outside and we opened the magic purse of deep
purple bedclothes
to climb in naked as a miracle
and I took you to me and became opalescent with your touch
and nothing is too good for you
I am the Queen of Everything
and you are the King of Whatever You Feel Like at the Moment
and you smell like all dogs go to heaven
and we are a wild pair.
I watch your beautiful hands
as you roll a cigarette
I like the auburn curls below your belly
and as you talk I endeavor to decipher
the language and history of your feet
bless me now for there is no tomorrow

It's Late

It's late and
I know you're not coming
with your upset
and your smoking outside
and your moving from room to room
it's like finding a bat in the house

it's late now and I know
you're not coming over
and that's okay
but I still miss you
and I had said bring me ice cream
because it won't hurt my teeth
and you like it too
but you didn't hear me
lost in your own complaints

and then a message—
the phones aren't working right—
a message—
to take care of myself.
I miss you and you will be gone soon
and I will miss you

POSTCARDS FROM A WOUNDED BIRD

England
June 16th

Grasshopper—
making vegan gingerbread
thinking of you
and how I wish you to be:
self confident, kind, elegant
you only get to vote once, and you vote with your life... choose something
you really believe in, and live it as much, as daily, as fully as you can.
Vote with your life, it makes a difference
history and mystery are in the balance

it is raining here in the Cotswolds
frost in the meadow early, fuzzy green in the willows,
rose bushes and daffodils don't seem to mind a bit...

roses in profusion
pink and red
rooks and carrion crows
cool air bird song
train sings through the golden valley
going places I don't want to go
no not going anywhere
bright eye over the fields
and ribbons of grey stone walls, a chorus of sheep in the low field

my heart is breaking, and why not?
the new one is so much bigger
it must have burst its seedcase
watered with tears
will this breaking and growing never end?
when your time is no longer forever you will think of me
your bed is an altar

every lovemaking
is an offering to the goddess
she always accepts this offering
in one of her many guises
tonight I am sad
and I can't be sad
it's too much, too much
'better to see god in everything than to try to figure it out'
anchored in unknowing
my heart is breaking

TEN POUND NOTE

In England, thinking of you
and certain small betrayals
when a jackdaw landed on the rail over my right shoulder
 I was cleaning cottages
on a day of no money at all
 I found a 10 pound note under the big chair
crows cawing in the treetops
at the bottom of the early summer field
thank you

ON A DAY OF SPECIAL MAGIC

Mid August in England
when Summer begins to make little leaving noises
and moves towards the door
on a day of special magic
gathering rose canes along the badger path
saying thank you to all the ancient trees in the high field
I thought — it's not feathering season for gathering by humans
and I thought — if there could be just one feather it would be
    so nice
I would send it to you
[this is that feather]
[magpie]
In these wild places
where everything runs like tiny perfectly chaotic clockwork
and crumble and decay are woven into the fabric of birth and rebirth
so closely as to be indistinguishable from each other
and small things happen quickly
and large things happen slowly
and the breath of a stone is immeasurable
in human years
the veil between the kingdoms of earthly nature and
earthly magic are as intertwined as the strands of a beaded curtain

FRANCE

I am in France very near the sea
Gypsy girls and apricot trees
sunshine moonshine
throw them in the pot
apricot jam is what we got
you stole a kiss...
please give it back

Waiting for a Hurricane

Today has been a very busy day
somewhere else
my grandmother's pearls lie in a drawer
my dog is lying on a couch
my friends are lying low

here
I do laundry
and bake a cake
and in a last desperate attempt to feel normal
I go out to the apple tree
and pick apples for the donkeys

I feed them apples
scratch their ears
and then run up the road with a bucket
and pick ALL the raspberries
and ALL the blackberries
until my hands are stained with the blood
of a thousand berries
and my legs are alive with nettleburn

fruit full
bloody and burning
I turn back to the farmhouse
back to the farmhouse
I am waiting for a hurricane
somewhere else.

SONO CLANDESTINA

I am in London. Tim paid the Gypsies their 600 pounds. His mother is barely speaking to me. I don't have appendicitis. My father is still alive. I am at Susan's house near the park and have just slept for fourteen hours. New Orleans is hotter and wetter than hell right now and I want to go home but may have to wait until September.

Going to the crossroads of Hecate in the old deer park I make an offering, runes and piss and apple seeds. It feels like home under the trees when it is dark and nearly raining...hello Hecate my love; please touch me gently that I may gently touch. Is this my work? To bear illness and sorrow, to encourage, to pray, to feed, to kiss. To forgive? Is this my work? To sit by the pond where my dog Rania Dzukel swam just four years ago, before my rings went into the river; before, and now it's after and there is no dog, only the love for a dog and I am still homeless and it's still okay as long as everything doesn't get lost and I am confused and have been seriously ill for nearly three weeks and don't want to give a shit sample at the hospital and Americans are the only people who have to pay for medical care in Britain because the British [and everyone else] have to pay for care in the USA.

So - what?

The park gate smells of foxes, its cool today, with rain coming, rain for a week, and five spotty downy ducklings are at the bench by the pond ...all saying peep peep peep peep. Peep.

It is Sunday, and I am walking down Richmond Hill to the river, I pass the old soldiers home and the memorial bench for Romero. I pass Pete Townsend's girlfriends car and stand with a tall German couple watching boats on the river Thames in the far distance, an aspect unchanged for thousands of years. I wonder about smuggling acorns across the border. Could I take all this with me to keep me strong and full of the smell of trees and rain and inflexible Old England with a heart of oak and gold; England, ashamed of past cruelty, unsure how to change, tolerantly observing the new or aberrant. What is this feeling of cool and calm? Safe, well fed, I want to

73

memorize this deep in my cells, deep blood bones, as a currency for days of hot agitated fear and plain poor food.

There is a Zydeco band playing, down by the river, I hear it first on the wind and cannot believe what I am hearing, Zydeco at the river Thames and it breaks my heart...entertaining people on the lawn and at the pubs. When will it be safe to cry? New Orleans is nearly dead and I want to go home and cry, but I am homeless. Swans and black clouds, boats on this English river, and down by the pub, zydeco, Louisiana zydeco.

It has been said, "what would you do if you knew you would live forever?" I think I might relax, and begin many things, and not hurry anything, and enjoy everything as much as possible; not hurry up to die, but slow down to live forever. Not worry, because tomorrow is another day, and you would know that tomorrow really would be another day, never the end of the world...Mississippi Ma, I am sick, and should probably go to the hospital.

Down at the riverside, sitting on a bench outside the Slug and Lettuce, no money for drink or food...

narrowboat, narrowboat how loverly you float
on the river — scullers, boats for hire, kayak flock.
at my feet — cigarette butts, goose feathers, drinks straws,
    old lemon slices, elm seed pods
this is one of my favorite spots on earth
humbled
not sure what to do yet
cashed that dollar
waiting for change
I look downriver
and think how nice it would be
to crawl to the bottom
and sleep forever
simple warm complete
I am lonely, lost
and have to be out by Thursday

DON'T START [crying]
everybody's cutting back
there is bread but no circus
I miss New Orleans
where it's all circus all the time.
Let go of all the other days
here are woods full of wild anemone
primroses and chestnut trees
there is only this day to begin.

It's cold, and the river smells of diesel. Seeing the first leaves of autumn here is a reminder of my brother David, bright blue eyes, rowing me out this way in a little wooden boat, some years ago when we were that much younger, when the world was new but it had been a difficult birth. Past the Violet Ellen, the All's Well, the Chrysalis...whose pretty boats are these? I like the beautiful wooden boat houses best. I could live there...

Swans dive for food, their lovely necks disappearing underneath, bodies like feathery footstools sitting on the water. It's hardly been summer here this year, scant sunshine, cold and damp.

A few hundred yards further down and the air is much better, with the smell of wood smoke hanging over the water. There is a slight drizzle as promised, and a cold wind in the flat boat rocking on the body of the river. The river holds a million secrets, including my dark amethyst wedding rings, in its deep...it's all still very green despite the chill, only mid August.

Boats For Hire
Richmond- Teddington Lock- Richmond
5 pounds
3pm
Last Time Out Today.
Just me, the boatman, and his lady.

BURGUNDY ST.

I rely on the wild card
I believe in miracles
ghostly apparitions made
of the scent of satsuma blossoms
church bells in the distance
through warm evening rain
and white crepe myrtle
glowing in early evening light.
Why am I alone
on this full moon evening?
waiting for someone else to come to their senses
or maybe
I am simply holding space
my real job
holding space
like those guys in the caves
I am a junior apprentice fucking space holder
me and the cat and the crepe myrtle
and one tiny satsuma
on a little satsuma tree
blooming its little heart out
for one tiny fruit
in a big pot on the balcony

and how lovely it is
on a gently rainy July night
full moon in New Orleans
I love the feel of warm rain on my bare legs
white wine bread and goats cheese
somewhere else there's a party
and somewhere else
someone's mad lover builds a space ship
ask me- I will go anywhere about now...
it is all driving me crazy
and there wasn't very far to go.

Someone was shot a few streets from here
just two nights ago
what were his dreams like
the night before the night?
did he know to put his soul in order?
Oh satsuma tree
may you live long and prosper
the scent of your little cream flowers
the sight of your one tiny fruit
and curled up in the pot
an orange cat

satsuma ripens
satsuma drops
hail
the turning

I seem to be so well hidden
why?
pretty boys on their silent bicycles
glide past beneath this balcony
they lock their bikes
an old man lets them in, across the street
a train whistle not too distant
why isn't someone letting me in?
I am here in the rain
holding space for Palestine
for Israel
for Detroit
for the mad scientist
for the children
I am in my cave
waiting for it all to go one way or another
it's raining softly
and I don't want to go inside
here is the nighttime UPS truck
        here's the cat sat on the mat
        sunset

in bright fading light glowing
on   houses at the end of the street
saying
no more rain soon

tomorrow is a market day
I sell good wishes
you need them
this should be a good day.

Friday/full moon/July 2014
New Orleans/balcony
Burgundy St

JOURNEY OF A THOUSAND MILES

Wed Mar 4, 2009

I left my room on Rampart Street driving a small U-Haul truck to a $38 a month storage locker on South Carrollton, Doc Otis and Louis Ledford riding shot gun. We arrived ahead of a brewing storm to find I'd left the keys on a windowsill...had the locks cut off by security and purchased 2 more. L and O filled the elevator w valuables, found elevator was broken ['UP' button had been savagely beaten], Security said we'd have to use the stairs, because they were "not an electrician, sorry".

Long story short, combining Otis's spatial manipulation skills, Louis good nature, and my magical thinking we managed to fit the elephant in the shoebox. Sweat, no blood no tears...later on, Louis said that was the best beer he ever tasted. I drove the U-Haul back to its stable and Otis followed in my van. By then it was getting dark. I dropped him off on Montegut Street with the furniture I forced him to borrow for his new Habitat for Humanity house, almost ready.

Two days after I bought Amzie's big green van, someone threw a brick through the street side back window. That was months ago. I don't usually let things go til the last possible moment but now something had to be done before the coming storm and before being parked for six months. Stopped at the hardware store on Elysian Fields and bought three big rolls of green duct tape and they gave me a heavy plastic contractor's bag. Lovely.

Off to the Sweet Olive B&B in the cold wind...

They let me in. I was oh SO bedraggled and stinky but could not lose momentum. Dave came out to the van and helped me get started with the window patch. Suitcases were hauled inside and I took a shower. Called Lord David at the Skull club across the street, looking for: 1.drink 2.food 3.ironic conversation, but he wasn't there so I ate leftover hummous and crackers from the Sweet Olive kitchen, drank the last glass of Chablis from a screwtop jug and was asleep in the Magnolia Room by 7:30 pm.

Thu Mar 5

Bed by 7:30 = up at 4 am.... brrr COLD. Hair in dreads, not on purpose. Too cold to wash. Find old coffee in kitchen, heat in micro w/ soymilk left chilling on bed room floor. Don't ask. Find heat setting on a/c. Yay! warm and packing to go. Nap/pack/nap. Pack, doorbell. Miss Clara knocks on the door of The Magnolia Room, Jelly Sandwich enters bundled up like a ...cold New Orleanian. NOLA winter clothes tend to be in very good condition and completely out of fashion due to not getting much wear. Jelly looks great at 7am and has brought me a present, a beautiful knitted hat and accessories, purple fluffy cone head fits right over my hair. She made them herself, and now my ears are warm so I drive her back to Decatur Street, and kiss bye bye.

What am I going to do with the van? The window is taped up, and I have to go. My friend said she'd take me to the airport and I could leave the van at her house til Otis gets his Habitat place. Better tell him that, soon. Meanwhile Clara can't wait to get me out of the house, since she's had Mardi Gras people nonstop for the past few weeks, so she was very helpful with suitcases.

Me and my friend and her elderly dog [who has no teeth, and leaves a bruise when she bites] bundle into her car, off to airport, kiss bye.

Flight to Houston ok, flight to California cancelled, might get on next flight out, might have to spend the night in Houston, will not know until 5 minutes before flight leaves... Yay! Off to California...vodka/tonic $5

Mar 5
California is the place of my childhood, with the ocean smell of seaweed, boats rocking on their tethers in the marina, seagulls only use their outside voices...great to see two of my kids, we are all at Sura's apt. in Marina Del Rey. 1 big cat, 1 little dog. Weather cool and bright.
Empty Nest Syndrome hit me pretty hard, soon replaced by No Nest Syndrome. Sura and Judah both in L.A. now... dinner tonight, cuddle, wear each others clothes. Yeah.

Mar 6
Oh, I know what it means to miss New Orleans...I miss you I miss you I miss who I am when I am with you...but I really do need: 1. boyfriend 2. regular income 3. a real place to live.
So if you miss me too, it's really not asking too much. I am very loyal

80

and deeply trustworthy,

adaptable yet principled. Maybe I'll go to www.caretaker.com, and see what's up, because I used to own property and I am the kind of person I would have wanted to keep an eye on things -

Female/old enough to know better/no smoke/no drugs/no pets/fascinated by sparkly stuff/poetic in tooth and claw/onomatopoeic to a fault.

Mar 8
Spring forward
Fall back
LAX 9AM
feels like 8
or maybe 10
my suitcase weighs 49 1/2 lbs
the limit is 50
I'm GOOD
teeny tiny airplane seats
huge sweet black man
big old white lady
man sleepy
lady in pain
me in the middle
to paraphrase from Groucho
relaxation is not possible
so I will just have to be relaxed anyway.

Mar 9
Bacon Hill Inn...babies have grown into children and where there were
    once dogs there is now a puppy.
Even snow flakes, in their supposedly infinite variety, are yin and yang
today's snowflakes: yin
yin is larger wetter and melts sooner.
The last time I slept in this room I was married
I remember the last meal he cooked in this house
I am afraid when I remember but that memory is strangely clearer to me
than memories of times I have been here since then
I am closing my eyes
Run through this, Magic Pony

Run for your life!
I am holding on to your sparkling mane
and you are magic pony running like the wind
just fly me to the kindest shore.

Mar 12
I am spending a week at the big farmhouse bed and breakfast run by Tim
and Katie. Katie is my foster daughter. She met Tim when we lived on
Bourbon Street. This house was built a long time ago, by the first governor
of New York, who invented Wall Street in NYC, which used to be a
farmers market. I seem to have some sniffles.

Cold and starry on a clear night...last night the full moon shone in the
window of my little bedroom at the far end of the house, beyond the second
parlor. The moon was so bright I could not sleep. I saw Odin and his lost
eye, which is the moon.

Sometimes the journey is just to the coffee pot. It is still the journey.

Mar 14
This year in New Orleans, at the Radical Faery St Brigid Ball on Feb
3, I wore the costume Yemaya, Queen of the Sea. Stuffed animal goldfish
Nemo sat in my headdress representing the creatures of the water, also
because the color at the Ball this year was orange. At Bacon Hill Inn I was
inspired to make a large Stick Dakini Dancer doll, "Yemaya Pregnant Waters
Dancing". As the doll was being assembled a big water pipe broke in the
basement, water rose to 4 feet. Tim discovered it and fixed it over the
next few days.

Spent 1 lovely pre-spring day in the hammock — 2 women 2 children 1
dog. Then off to Penn Station, water main broken! had to go overland on
foot to Grand Central with Stephanie and Chance, 2 women 1 child 2 fifty
pound suitcases up and down stairs all around the town. At last safely home
in the little Brooklyn apartment with my son Lucas and his family, cuddled
on the couch again, tonight... overseas tomorrow.

Mar 15
Flight : no problem
England : green
Sprig of overwintered thyme from the garden
in a cup of hot water for my coldy-ness, sitting on terrace bench, view

of the Golden Valley.

Spring is springing at Westley Farm! Buds are budding, little birds tweeting and twittering bulbs and forest flowers flowering. The air is kind and crisp, box hedge green and glossy in the knot garden 4 hearts 3 diamonds 4 clipped gooseberry trees and a plinth and daffodils in profusion in the lawn.

Turn turn the wheel of the year turn turn again. I have now begun growing old and its alright here on the bench with my black umbrella to shade me from the brightness.

Here in Chalford alone in the garden I have walked through that crone-ing gate [which opened the day after my last birthday] I find myself just fine and actually quite at home, in a feisty old way, in my blue cotton dress and my black army boots and my hair several unlikely shades of red...

Tattoos and age spots my jewelry is real gold
I have no fixed abode and a very small bank account
If I can hold on and have fun for another 25 years I will have aced it.
Turn turn but oh turn slowly please
I like this life I've been working on
I think I'm starting to get the hang of it...

Mar 25

Jessica and Saskia drive off to see Susan , who is blooming and piano free, feeding birds and feathering her nest. We will also to get the Middle East Report from David Grimes who is in London briefly on a mission from God [ess]..and who must go to Liberty's of London for ladies handkerchiefs to replenish the supply of friend in Alaska.

David recently returned from an ancient cave of Pan in the wilds of Israel, working with Artists For Nature, counting every migrating bird who was willing to participate and had a note from home.

View of Thames from Richmond Hill- gloriously bright.

Liberty's — amazing as always and more expensive than ever.

DG finds hankies. I find a small rare sewing tool, much needed in the doll making business,[3 pounds] I also find tiny potential fairy crowns of gold and silver butterflies,[2 pound 50 per roll].

Not expensive....priceless.

Rain. Long coffee at Oxford Circus. Middle East Report concluded.

World peace imminent, land mines avoided by sticking to cow path and watching for sadly exploded cows of which there were none. We return to Susan's exhausted, I am still not completely well but getting better. Lie down for an hour, get up and cook tarragon chicken in white wine mushroom sauce w jasmine rice and winter squash, spring salad of rocket [arugula], cucumber, watercress, littlegem lettuce.

Saskia arrives back from Brighton smelling of woodsmoke and with a mysterious look in her eye.

Dinner over, back to the Cotswolds Westley Farm. 2 hours 45 min... no hurry.

Apr 1

Today out walking 6 dogs, me and my friend Robbie down through the field behind Rinky Dinks, down to the flowing spring where dogs can drink and bathe, to the old stables, one brick wall and a stone floor... I pour out a libation for horses gone before...wood anemones daffodils pretty little forest flowers buds and birdsong...

We have elderflower presse and 2 books and lay under the bare trees with their little lacy dresses of new ivy.

Dogs are dogging.
I believe that the earth is alive and that it sings in each one of us
I believe in kindness
to others and to myself
I believe that animals tell our story to the gods when they die
and that their stories are counted when we die
I believe that laughter and food and sex are holy mysteries and that holy
    mystery should be the rule
rather than the exception
I believe that the wool of a black sheep
is just as warm

April 12

Happy Ishtar...Hege made wonderful beautiful little Easter baskets for each member of the household. Julian is making dinner. Tara is arranging the Roving Studio, her big blue traveling truck, out in the barn. Emma is in London. Robbie is at his house with Paddy and the dogs. Saskia is in Brighton at the allotment squats and I kind of wish I was too, even though I don't really know yet what's going on there. It's been weird being sick for a whole month of traveling/visiting. However, I am feeling a lot better now.

Sometimes I just long to go home, but there isn't one. A peaceful place, safe, to put things and to grow things, for people to visit me, to cook and clean and think deep thoughts... who knew it would come to this?

When Martin left me I had some money. I ran away from England, back to New Orleans and bought a place, putting all money into that property...the house made it through Hurricane Katrina, and then burned down 5 months later. I had to pay the mortgage etc. anyway, even though there was no house, and no business. I was badly injured in post-Katrina wreckage. Insurance money insufficient, ripped off by contractor. Beginning of mortgage crisis. One year to rebuild. Couldn't re-mortgage. Sold to pay debts. Bankrupt. Home-free.

I am willing. I am kind. I am treasure. I am making dolls and writing poems. Someone has to do this work.

Magic, Music and Beautiful Clothes...very important. Carry on. Alright. Spring into summer.

April 30

Trip to Brighton...I have bought an old wooden fife, black with a bit of silver. Rob drives me to see Saskia in her current spot on Earth. He will see his old running buddy Hilaire. People living on the allotments [public food garden land] in sheds, trailers, tents, semi permanent camp on a green cliff overlooking the very beautiful city of Brighton, with a view of the harbor and ocean.

Saskia making flower essences from a little shed next to Hilaire who has been there amazingly and sort of illegally for 14 years. He has built many veg beds and beautiful fences. There is a fire pit and a pot full of laundry. Lots of dirty dishes. Two big white chickens, the male has a mutated double comb and extra toes, very handsome. Bock. Peck.

Children have been visiting, scattered paint and flower art projects ...two little dogs chase down paths and under hedges.

Saskia lights a fire in her woodstove. We sit in her shed, drink vodka and laugh. Her bed is fluffy and every shade of magenta purple. The floor is stacked high with beer boxes because Hilaire's birthday party is coming up and she is trusted not to start drinking it....the men are at his shed smoking and talking crazy talk while Hilaire sits at his little table clipping paper, making the seed shapes of sacred geometry. Leftover dinner from the pot. Camp sleep.

The next morning is sunny and warm, and I make coffee, walk around and play my fife. People garden and wash dishes. Three of us and one little dog go raggle taggle to the seaside, lie on the pebbly beach, and wade in the tide pools, picking up shells and chalk pieces. After seaside cafe tea and cake, a walk through the town, Infinity Food store and the public gardens by the Pavilion. They still have elm trees, saved from Dutch elm disease, [a weeping elm, perhaps because all those other elms died]... maybe Saskia could make weeping elm medicine, for those who carry on in strength and beauty.

We pile into the little truck with our food and seaside treasures, and roll back up the hill to the allotments. As night falls Hilaire makes lamb/barley/veg stew and mashed potatoes, mashing them up gorgeously with butter in the big pot outside...Me and Rob and Saskia relax on Hilaire's bed which is the only place to sit in the little shed as he alternately cooks and clips paper, sacred geometry seeds everywhere. Some food comes from the skip [dumpster], some is grown, some is bought or donated. There is smoke and beer. People from all over the world drift by, Dutch Nigerian Polish Tibetan ...I sing "Sammy's Bar". More camp sleep.....AM coffee and food and everybody eats, and I like that...playing my fife, practice "The Boys of Mullabawn", a great old tune, don't remember how I learned that a million years ago in Ireland or Indiana. Saskia announces that it is a Flower Day, washes her hair, puts on a dress and makes a new essence. For me it is a drive away day, back to the Cotswolds. Essence delivery. Thank You.

WHITE NOISE MACHINE

I have a white noise machine
it helps me sleep by playing
what are called "soothing sounds"
designed to cover up the unsoothing sound
of downstairs neighbors tv at 2 am
or drunks on the street
or fellow travelers rolling in at 4.
There are many sounds to choose from
but they all sound strange to me.
The "spring rain" setting sounds like bacon frying
and that wakes me up
"mountain stream" sounds like the toilet is running
that wakes me up
there is a setting called simply "white noise"
but it sounds like someone forgot to turn off the tv and of course
that wakes me up.
The only setting I like is called "ocean waves"
I like it very much
it is very soothing.
I sleep well, dreaming of the beach and beautiful drunken surfers
with portable tvs.

CONVERSATIONS WITH MYSELF

abandon hope
let go
abandon despair
let go:
uncertain
willing
generous

Rumi says, "sit, be still, and listen
because you are drunk
and we are at the edge of the roof"
and I say
God bless us all whom the Muses have stunned

I am stunned

"shatter your illusions on the rock of truth"

I am shattered

gather your roses while you may
these same flowers
tomorrow will
be compost

"don't be afraid of me, I'm just like you"
what? lonely? wild? unsettled?
delicate, strange, slightly deranged?
frightened?
too cool for school?

my life is full of questions right now—
like
where are my other sunglasses?

why do I get leg cramps?
at what point do tattoos stop being sexy?
my friend, if you are just like me,
we are both in trouble.
I say
a blessing on you whom the muses have stunned
as you drink till the pain goes away

Zorba the Greek says
if a woman asks a man to her bed
and he refuses,
it is a sin in the eyes of God.

My friend said
this is the oldest joke in the world
"a man, a woman, and a snake walk into a bar"

it has been said
"take what is worth keeping,
and with the breath of kindness
blow the rest away."
and all that is worth keeping is
who I have become when YOU are blown away
you
like a husk
and me,
lost
beautiful flowering floating free...

and a blessing on you
whom the muses have stunned
as you drink
till the PAIN just goes away

and a blessing
on the parents and friends and the lovers and children
all caught in the games that you play
for the bright shining light

and the fight
and the flight
and the hearts that are broken alone in the night
and bless your fucking moods
and your comforts
and your discomforts
and your absence   and your absence
your absence.

abandon hope
abandon despair
save yourself
uncertain
willing
generous

ANGRY MOON

I have danced naked in the moonlight
covered with mud
and my own menstrual blood
I have howled at the desert moon
hair matted
eyes wild
body turned to leather by the sun
I have spat snakes
and sung a primal song of birth and death
and rebirth
I have pounded my feet in the dust
I have lusted and been satisfied
and lusted and been made furious by deprivation
I have worshipped madness and the thin line
I have embraced sorrow
with a fierce hateful joy
as though
if it trusted me
I might get closer
and stab it in the heart

now can you love me?
can you love my oldest song?
are you great? are you greater?
one look at me can turn you to dust
I am angry fierce beautiful as the desert plain
dancing
dancing
snake dancing
wedded to the sun
I am the angry moon
with nothing of my own
but the mad power of reflection

THE DEATH OF MY BROTHER

grief
horrible agonizing
paralyzing cavernous grief
sick mad screaming
intruding clawing insidious
languishing
grief
grief unending overwhelming
stabbing wracking noxious
absolute utter hopeless grief
and it's
sorrow sorrow
to my heart
since I and my brother did part
oh you pale slender child
deep brown eyes long lashes
deep soul brother eyes
little head little hands
pale pale pale skin
awkward the grief of our mother
our father never spoke your name again
Eastertime
our mother silently opened windows
airing the empty room
and still and small
you blew away forever
forever
with the breeze
in white curtains

I Look For You

My brother died when he was six
I am resigned
I never look for him
I know his voice is in my heart
I know I'll never see him anymore

you died when you were twenty eight
a suicide
and I still look for you
I look in crowded streets
in cafes, in the shops

I look for you
as if you might appear at any moment
and when I see a certain friend
I stare
because he looks like you
and he is growing old with me

I only want to see
that flash of you
in him
the way you might have held your head
or turned to greet me or a friend
I stare at him because he looks like you
he's all I have of you
you died when you were twenty eight
but I still look for you

I look for you in your exquisite child
she doesn't really look like you
but your shadow falls across her life
coloring everything she is
or does or wants to be
with your absence

I look for you
and find you missing
I look for you
you must be here
 I see your shadow everywhere

WALKING BY THE SHORE IN MY THIN BLACK COAT

It's November
we are staying in an old stone house
in a room with windows that look out over the sea
there is a fire in our room
but the rest of the house is empty

the sea is cold and grey
everything outside is foggy
the wind is wild
and forces itself between my ribs

under my clothes
sometimes I am fat and yellow
now I feel very small and white

I was longing for this weather
I was longing for an obvious source of chill
you are here
my heart is still warm
but some terrible cold thing has frightened me
perhaps if we go back to our room
my tears will thaw and spill

Bi Incarnate

people are bi-sexual, bi-racial,
bi-coastal, bi-lingual
I am   bi-incarnate
all beauty and untimely...
human, djinn
   angel
taken not returned
born speaking tree and bird.
I don't know anything.
There are no long books in me
I will open this door or that gate
and say hello
waiting between breaths
we are untimely
waiting in the wild places
I stand in the doorway and look back

in Japan, by law,
perfect employment for the bi-incarnate
a portal to the Otherworld must be tended
in every city center.

AT FIRST I THOUGHT
MY CAT WAS DEAD

Feb 2013

Waking in the cool New Orleans morning
from deep dreaming sleep
I am inexplicably convinced that my cat has died.
Suddenly a tiny bottle of van van oil jumps off the shelf
and uncorks its voodoo self, spilling across the room.
Dreaming,
I dreamt I was holding you,
and you were talking
[all the years you talked and I was fascinated]
and I realized, finally,
that I was bored.
I said, speaking gently into your ear
from right behind you
"You know what, I'm not in love any more."
Naked, warm, and feeling your smooth body
spooned in front of mine
I held you close
as I had done so many
many times before.

BLEED SORROW

When you left me my heart was shattered into a million pieces
I want to grind those pieces into a fine sharp dust
to sprinkle in your food
to interfere with your digestion
and in your eyes as you lie sleeping
so you cry out in pain as you wake up.
Pulverized shattered heart can be very dangerous
you shouldn't have done that.
I will use our money
to pay the maid in a strange hotel
to scatter it in your bed,
even though she has offered to do it for free.
Little shards of broken heart will become embedded in your palms
and then, when you go to the bed of your lover
as you caress her body
the splinters will work deeper into your hands
and you will bleed sorrow onto everything you touch.

The stain is difficult to remove

BONFIRE

the bed is the altar of the night
the table is the altar of the day
I will put on my blue dress and go down to the river
I will give her my heart
I have nowhere else to go
she takes broken things
she doesn't ask questions
I want to cut
to draw blood
everything hurts

I was crying
'do you still love him?'
[he said]
no
I said
but this charred bonfire
of mutilated angels speaks for itself

St Roch punk and monkey show
in case of emergency I will break this
glass

run away run away run away now
I ran away many years ago
I ran away
before you were born, beloved
and I am still away
I joined the circus
I am a gypsy
I am a pirate queen
I am the Peace Corps
I am bright and wild
I am not an island
I ran away to show you where away is
it is only to be found at the center of the map
the map of the heart
I am waiting for you
in the secret hiding place
living on faith and shadows
hope and starlight
on the run
 with Tinkerbelle and Bob Marley
Beatrix Potter, Helen Hill
Jack Sparrow, Galadriel
your real father
and you and me
you are your own treasure map
run away run away run away now
we'll all have tea
in the secret hiding place at the center of the heart
where we can love
with no therefore

FOR MY SON LUCAS ON HIS BIRTHDAY

Tomorrow is your 23rd birthday
this morning I went up on Glastonbury Tor
and picked wild grasses for you
far away
and the stem of horse chestnut leaves
I spread my black coat on the hillside
and laid on my back
looking at the sky
thinking of you
feeling the ancient air
a flock of sheep grazed it's way around the hill
eating grass and the little magic mushrooms that dance
in wet sprouty spots on the green slope

you are 23
Glastonbury Tor is several thousand
I love you a million billion
maybe it's good to be thought about in a magic place
I think of you a lot
just in case

ALTERCATION 2010

Because your name means trouble,
yesterday you had no name
your name was beauty
soft and glad
dolphin woman
your name is gentle, real and blessed
wounded, soft and blessed

WILL

Henna red, sleepy head
dreaming on an English afternoon
Piaf slept outdoors in the daytime
on the streets of Paris.
I remember living on the purple sidewalks of Chicago
and the psychedelic street salons of the Haight.
Here you are asleep on a bench
in this sleepy place,
resting in the rare dim sunlight of the Cotswolds
wrapped in your ratty leather jacket
with my straw bag under your head.
I play with diamonds
South African a hundred years ago
throwing catching scattering light
making rainbows on the white
page and in the air.
I watch the sunlight on your hennaed hair.

FREAKY PAUL

"I can laugh about myself, my work, the universe,
because I know what serious really is."
—Ninotchka Rosca

My parents decided to get divorced after I brought Freaky Paul home on Thanksgiving Day. It must have been the last straw, the last brick in the walled up room of my mother's heart, a room in which my father was no longer welcome and which no man would ever see again. I was fourteen.

Freaky Paul was my friend. He was seventeen. He had been beaten really badly and had some brain damage, but he didn't start out that way. The year before, when he was sixteen years old, he hitch hiked alone to the Grand Canyon. He camped by himself for two weeks alone in a cave at the bottom of the Grand Canyon. I asked him what he ate, and he said peanut butter sandwiches. He wasn't there to eat. He played music on a strange instrument he'd built - something like a harp made on an old guitar body. He played space music - delicate, weird, lovely- fasting, sixteen years old, alone at the bottom of the Grand Canyon.

He wanted to tell me about it. He really needed someone to understand how important those two weeks had been.

Sometime later, having hitch hiked back to the city, he was walking down the street near his parent's house. A gang of boys jumped him and beat him up. They beat him so badly that after he got out of the hospital his face looked different, and he forgot things, and his speech was difficult to understand.

I met Freaky Paul down on 57th Street where a lot of us very young white bohos liked to hang out. He was already freaky when I met him, and I never knew him any other way...curly brown hair, medium build, shy silly smile, still pretty even though his face was kind of squashed. Pale brown eyes, sometimes alarmingly blank; layers and layers of clothes...great big

104

shoes. He was gentle, and constantly delighted by his musical discoveries. His train of thought was kind of hard to follow, but his attitude was great, as thought always seemed to lead to quiet amazement.

People didn't really understand - he thought really deeply, and considered things. I guess he did have brain damage, but somehow we were on a similar wavelength. He didn't think things simply because he was supposed to think them. He thought things that occurred to him, and everything was new and worth examining.

I was fifteen and it was August, and the sidewalk was hot. Long days, stifling nights, young hopeful mornings. An occasional thunderstorm would crack open the humidity and the city could breathe a sigh of relief. I used to go barefoot in the summertime, all over the city, a skinny uncombed kid in costume rags, barefoot on the train, down the alleys, on the corner panhandling for dimes, up the worn burgundy carpet stairways of those old wood cabbage dinner cool tile brownstones.

Twelve cents would buy a giant pickle floating embryonically in electric green pickle juice, hermetically sealed in a plastic pouch. I learned to like pickles. Everything was new, everything was marvelous.

I wasn't exactly looking for guys. I was on a mission, I was looking for souls, kindred spirits, the ones like me. So when Freaky Paul showed up all shuffling and talking funny, me and him became an occasional gang of two.

The streets were ours... the cool oily smell of grime gusting out from under the train tracks; the cracks and colors of the sidewalks, all lavender and grey to me. We lived there, sitting on the curb, feet in the gutter, or hanging out in sympathetic shops or cafes.

Find a penny, pick it up, and all day long you'll have good luck. I was always available for errands. I liked to be sent out to pick up coffee and grilled cheese sandwiches for the guys at the head shop. It made me feel so ...grown up.

And then I'd get a tip. And then me and Paul would cross the street at the corner, and go push open a special heavy old door, quietly entering into an old fashioned, white tile and glass case chapel of sugar, fragrance and beauty - the donut shop. There was no place to sit inside, it was too small, almost literally a hole in the wall, tucked beneath the train trestle. They just made 'em and sold 'em. The elderly German guy behind the counter would cheerfully take our fourteen cents and hand over two jelly donuts and two napkins and we would say thanks and be back outside on the street in a flash. He was nice to us, courteous. He treated us like we were real people, he handled our money like it was real money.

That was the summer, such a long summer. Time passes slowly for young people. Slowly the weather began to change, days grew shorter, the wind off the lake grew cold and it rained. It wasn't always so wonderful to be outside.

End of November, Thanksgiving Day. My parents wanted me to eat dinner with the family at home. If home was really where the heart is, and if the family was really the ones who knew you best, then I would have spent the afternoon eating bean tacos near the tracks on Howard Street, with four or five of my closest friends, none of whom had a last name.

So, I took Freaky Paul home with me. He had parents somewhere, maybe they were drunk or something. Anyway, he didn't seem to have anywhere to go. It was a grey day, soft and quiet, the kind of day that can feel either cozy or depressing depending on your frame of reference. We took the train up and walked from the station.

My sister answered the door. Paul waited in the front hall, standing in his big lace up leather shoes and his worn wool coat, carefully setting his wonderful musical instrument down on the bench. It smelled so good in that house. I went into the kitchen to find my mother. She wiped her hands on her apron and followed me back into the hall.

I asked her if Paul could eat with us, because he didn't have anywhere else to go, and she was very nice to him and she said yes.

My father did not say yes. He was very angry and he said no. He didn't want an unfamiliar terribly hurt bundle of oddities seated at his family table.

My mother quietly went into the kitchen and cut into everything she had cooked. She piled a plate with turkey and gravy and dressing and green beans and fruit salad and pumpkin pie, and me and her and Freaky Paul sat in the front hall, on the bench at the bottom of the stairs, and he took off his coat and ate the food. He ate as much as he could, and thanked my mother, and played me a little short weird piece of music on his weird musical instrument, and then pulled his coat back on and headed out into the November night. In the kitchen, my mother cried. Then we all sat down to dinner.

Not long after that, while my father was out of town on business, my mother left that house. My brothers helped her move, in the big brown econoline van they used to haul band equipment. She took what she thought was hers.

Out on the street in early spring, not quite budding time, but bird coming back time, and taking stock of winter damage time...I couldn't find Freaky Paul. He hadn't been around for awhile, and no one had seen him. Someone knew where his parent's house was. A few days later, we all knew how those guys had beat up Freaky Paul again, and some body found him and took him to the hospital, and this time he just didn't make it. Just like that.

I buried him. I buried him in my heart, in a special place, no one could ever know.

I think of him and his strange music. His feet didn't touch the ground, and his beautiful little damaged heart was as fine as a feather.

Why would anyone want to hurt him?

I guess maybe his wings were showing; wings, coming out of the back of that old coat, and some people thought it was just too freaky.

I Love You, Anna

Once I lived on a commune made up of around fifteen to thirty households, depending on the season, repopulating a small rural town in the Midwest. We commune dwellers were not on the same wavelength as most of the original inhabitants of the tiny town, and they often let us know it, but some of us were friendly with some of them, and the dropout hippie heiress who funded the commune actually owned the whole town, so there we were.

I lived at first in a house that had been built from one of those four room Sears Roebuck mail order house kits that people used to be able to purchase from a catalog. The bundles would arrive by train, lots of bundles, all clearly marked, including plans and everything that was needed to build a simple house, or even more bundles and fancy stuff depending on what size house you could afford.

This was a plain little four room house with no plumbing. Its front porch was a concrete slab with a roof over it, held up by two turned wood posts, posts that Willie eventually painted with trompe l'oeil climbing vines. The property was shaded by a three hundred year old oak tree, the biggest fattest most wonderful tree for miles around, and there was an artesian spring down the hill in the back, a cool shady crack where watercress grew and time stood on tiptoe and the opinions of birds took on extra significance.

In the surrounding few miles, every formerly empty house or empty field was filled with the serious or frivolous, musicians and farmers, dirt poor scrapers, Vietnam vets, fortunate heirs, single parents, students, politicos, magicians, and seekers after stuff on every level. People built more houses, put up tipis, parked busses, planted crops, made babies, and pretty much got along.

I lived in that little four room house next to the big oak tree. I lived with Lucas, who was almost two years old, and five or six other people. My mother often came to visit, and she'd let me sleep in the morning, taking Lucas outside to sit on the edge of the porch playing in the sunshine, keeping him out of the road. It was high summer, when the locusts never stopped their song, and silence was unimaginable, and there was so much green that I just wanted to turn green too, and welcome the inevitable.

Faintly, from among the sounds of the early morning woods, half dreaming, I heard a strange "dank-dink-donk" sound over and over at regular intervals. The sound came closer gradually, and with it the sound of slowly moving trucks, and men's voices.

My mother sat on the porch hanging on to Lucas, as a curious procession wound slowly past, down the narrow country road. Several vehicles formed a line, with the Willys Jeep at the end. Romano stood in the Willys, wearing nothing but his overalls, big curly hair flying in all directions, banging on the bottom of an old sauce pan with a big wooden spoon, ultimately commanding the attention of a young buffalo. This orphan buffalo was somehow entranced by the "donk" sound of the spoon hitting the pan, and all the attention and parental guidance from a slowly moving herd of old trucks and skinny half dressed hippies.

This was the round up, pardner. They were heading home. Everybody waved, and Mom and Lucas waved back, "dink dank donk" past the house, and the oak tree, six o'clock in the morning, disappearing down the road.

This house was a little house, but it was like the house in your dreams where there is always some extra space that you've never seen before...and more things fit in it than ever could fit.

George came to stay, from somewhere far away, I think. He was dark and slender and Syrian or Greek or something. He had a big black mustache and he was gentle and intelligent and quiet and funny. I think he stayed in Jim's room. That's the kind of house it was, it only had four rooms but I never could figure out where George stayed. Jim sold occult books from a little shop up at the crossroads, next to the gas station and general store.

That fall I went away with a big caravan of buses, fifty vehicles all made into gypsy houses. Eventually this caravan would become The Farm, in Tennessee. Eighteen people slept in our bus, mostly on the floor. There was exactly enough room for everyone to lie down at night. I got mononudeosis,

109

and Lucas and I left for the city to be near my mother.

In April we came back to the commune, and moved in upstairs at the general store, waiting for it to get warm enough to live outside in a tent. The buffalo calf died that winter and up on a ridge in the woods its skull stood bleaching on a pole outside Seth's tipi. I used to have a large tent down the path from him, until it was burned by the KKK. I like a square home, I like to sleep in a corner. I like doors, and windows, and I like to have an altar on every wall.

There were good people in the general store house. Laurence lived there. He had a lot of windowpane LSD to sell. This acid was so pure that if you put your hand on the outside of the UPS box, the light in the room would change. It was so good you could almost see through the box. It was highly molecular.

For the first time in my life I had enough money to give some away. Sheila came up one day and asked if she could borrow five dollars, and I just gave it to her. She and her husband had twins, and two years later they had another child born on the twins birthday. It was a heady feeling for me to give some money away, and I really hoped she wouldn't mind. That five dollars has come back to me a thousand times. It was obviously a serendipitously sound investment.

George knew about a scheme where he could breed black widow spiders for the US government, which would pay handsomely for his contribution to the whatever-it-was effort. He thought it sounded like a legal, easy way to make money growing something at home, and he was talking about it to anyone who was interested.

He still lived in the little Sears Roebuck house, next to the big oak tree, with a lot of other people, including an odd and beautiful girl named Anna. Anna had pale skin and long thick dark hair, and a curvy womanly body. She didn't always finish her sentences, which didn't always turn out to be about anything, and it was hard to tell if she really liked me or not, but she was trying very hard to space in, from a very long way away, and she was beautiful, and really those things combined can make a person seem worthwhile.

There were some of those kind of rural pink and grey Christians who lived in their own community nearby. They made friends with Romano's wife by successfully helping to wean her little girl from the breast. That child was difficult, and no doubt it was a kinder and more deeply Christian effort than those goodish people realized, for creating a situation where an exhausted mother can get a full night's sleep is some fine bread cast upon excellent waters.

Once they had Romano's ear these Christians mentioned their chief concern about what was going on in our little community. Not nude swimming, or left-wing politics; not fornication, or the widespread use of marijuana.

No, it had to be witchcraft, proven by two obvious cases, one being me in my little room with the altars on the walls, holed up in there and then walking around the woods quiet for hours on end. The other being George, who, it was said, kept a room full of black widow spiders.

Romano assured these good people that they had nothing to worry about and suggested at a community meeting that both George and I might want to keep an eye out for marauding Christians.

One cold night in late April I woke up suddenly in the dark upstairs at the general store. The upstairs was quiet and deep asleep, and the night was under-the-trees, out-in-the-woods, no electricity dark, still and empty except for some little breathing sounds and a faint murmur of voices carrying from the room below. I stood like a sleepwalker and found my way to the top of the stairs, probably by the gentle glow of that box of windowpane, stopping to put two tiny crystals under my tongue, then slipping silently down the stairs, still half dreaming, ready to share who knows what with who knows who, in a swirling easy baroque night meeting.

In the warm fragrant room below, by the light of one candle, Jamie and Deborah were keeping their own vigil, tending a fire in the big woodstove. They greeted me, and I curled up quietly in my nightgown, in a soft chair close to the stove, and went back to sleep.

I woke up suddenly again. They both looked at me, and then they knew, because they were both people who knew things easily, and she looked at me and said, "what have you done?" and I looked at her and she said "when did

111

you do that?" I smiled a little more, I think, and then no more questions, just the kindness and ease of friendships forged through eons and momentarily touching in time and space. They made me put on a sweater. At some point she blew out the little candle which had been our only light, "to see," she said, "what would happen." With no light, the only source of illumination came from the red shadows outlining the door of the woodstove. The shadows began to roll and breathe, and soon filled the room, revealing the floating body of a big dark dragon, fifteen feet long, five feet high, circling the woodstove about three feet off the ground. It filled every air space in the room, with its head near me, floating hot and so deeply Saturnine as to be almost malevolent. Perhaps its heat came from the coldness of its eye. It was mine, though...not bad, not good, maybe a guard or a guide though I got some feeling that I could be sizzled at any moment. It was wonderful and scary and just as I began to get worried Deborah quietly lit the candle again, and all large floating unusual beings vanished, and she and Jamie looked at each other and said, "hmmm, that felt kind of strange" and I didn't say anything. When I finally spoke, I said, "I need to pee and there's too many wild dogs out there, somebody's got to go with me."

So Jamie went out into the night with me where the air was cold and clear, and there was a bright wet spring frost on the ground, and there were no dogs. We stopped by the side of the road, halfway between the general store and the three hundred year old oak tree. I squatted to pee on a slight rise in the ground, moving my feet apart so they wouldn't get wet. It was deep night and as quiet as frost and starlight and acres of trees can ever be. I stood up billowing slightly in the old sweater and my white nightgown and a pair of someone's big green rubber boots. We stood in silence for a long moment.

Then I thought of Anna. Anna who I couldn't understand. Anna who wanted to be one of us so much but was so far away in her own mind. Anna, dreaming, in the house by the oak tree, just down the road.

I looked wildly at Jamie. He put his arms around me and I began to cry. I wept hot and pure, from my deepest heart, and when I pulled away I looked into his eyes and they became Any Eyes Will Do, and I looked into his eyes and said, "I love you Anna, I love you, Anna, I love you, Anna," through his witness, but all for her, "I love you, Anna."

112

Anna and George fell in love. No, I think they arose in love. Anna adored him. He adored her. She began to speak in complete sentences. She floated, she was beautiful. He had to get a job and he was responsible. She was pregnant and they got married. They went to live in the city and they took a small apartment on the second floor of an old brownstone. George went out one winter evening to get a quart of milk at the corner store. A man came in to rob the store and stabbed George with a knife. He died. George died before the baby was born.

We love you, Anna.
We love you, Anna.

Deborah went to Europe with an international drug dealer. Jamie went to jail for three years and then moved to Hawaii. Romano got rich growing dope in Humboldt County. Willie played accordion in the Tom Waits band. Seth still has the buffalo skull. Sheila died in a car wreck. Her three boys joined the Marines. I went to live in England, and then came back. Anna disappeared.

Lucas bakes bread and lives in a house with lots of people. I think it's one of those houses you see in your dreams...the one that has more rooms than you ever knew, and more things fit in it than ever could fit.

BILL JONES

I saw Bill Jones and his wife
and their new foster child
inclining his head gently toward the child
he said "I asked for a teenager
and they sent me this"

she was about ten years old
midwest pretty
curly hair dancing step
eyes you could write a fiddle tune for

I gave her a flower from the brim of my hat
and told her "if you leave it out of water
it will dry into a perfect little rosebud
and then it will last forever"

she looked at me quietly
holding the red rosebud in her little white hand
eyes wide
she turned to Bill Jones
and said
"oh, but it's not open yet"

I Dreamed I Saw My Cat Last Night

In January, I dreamed I saw my cat, and whether she was alive or dead, I don't know, I only know that she was alright, and that I might not hear from her again. She almost died two years before, locked in a garage by mistake during a hard freeze, a cold spell lasting two weeks, and when she was found by the old man from across the street she was tiny, starved and filthy, but alive. He said to my foster child "is this your cat?" holding out the little wasted blinking bundle, his breath made a cloud between them, and she said "yes! oh yes, thank you!" and ran home with Ginger in her coat. For a while, we wondered if she would recover, but we cleaned her up and fed her people food and in a month or so she was as funny and oblivious as ever and ready to wander once again.

The following winter, she learned to speak. Her voice had always been an almost soundless short scratchy whine, maybe the bottom notes of a sound too high pitched to be heard by the human ear. That winter we left her in the care of a bass player, and she attached herself to him and somehow gained the gift of speech in so doing. I think his playing may have inspired her to modulate her voice for the human ear. When we returned in early spring, she said "meow", and ever after, although she continued to walk quietly and with an aura of perpetual deep minded distraction, and although she had a great detached disregard for most human activity, she would give us a "meow" in her moments of greatest need.

The winter of my dreaming she left for good, wandering in the high pale gold grass around the new house, two hundred acres shared with wild turkeys, possums and raccoons, and lots of little edibles in the bushes. She almost never came inside. She was the color of baskets, she liked the straw, she always had liked to disappear into things, chameleoning on top of the big basket in the hall, or in a game of cat/no cat here, just an old tan sweater on a yellow velvet chair.

It was January when I dreamt of her, seeing her clearly half hidden under a bush. The snow had melted but the earth was still frozen. There was a flicker, a pulse - was it within, or hovering, about to take flight? Was it a last word, or was it "here I am - see - a bush. I was your cat and I am still accountable to you." Perhaps she stretched and breathed a little steamy January cat breath, and stuck out her little pink tongue, and showed her perfect tiny sharp teeth in a yawn, and walked by herself [as they do] back to a dinner of mouse and a bed of straw, in the barn.

My Mother's Gun

I personally have only shot a gun once. I was living with my kids in a 1952 Alma travel trailer next to my friend Molly's house out in the country. My other friend Jimmy K liked Molly so much, he shot out the street light just for her. She hadn't asked him to do it, he simply wished to please her, since the new street light ruined the dark of night, stars and moonlight at Molly's beautiful tumbledown cabin. She came home one evening and the deed had been done, and of course she immediately realized the depths of his feelings for her. He hung around the house as much as he could, and one afternoon we had target practice out back, tin cans on the old fence and BLAM! I got to shoot a gun. That was fun.

This was different. One morning my mother called to tell me she was working for my ex boyfriend, the dope dealer with a heart of gold. She was a stash house. Someone had tried to break in through her kitchen door. She was scared, and decided she was going to have to buy a gun. Growing up in East Texas during the Depression, her father taught her how to drive and shoot at the age of 13, just like that song -"he let her drive the car when he's too drunk to." Mom hadn't actually had anything to do with guns or shooting since then, and she asked me to accompany her to the gun store, for moral support. I felt slightly guilty, being the link between her wanting a gun and my dangerous ex, so even though shopping for a pistol sounded like a horrible way to spend the day together, I agreed to go.

We parked in the hot weedy lot and entered a small cement block building at the back of a strip mall. Glass cases were full of guns and more guns. It was all very foreign and overwhelming to me, but my unshakeable mother knew just what she wanted, and the nice gun shop man helped her. They talked about how she should go practice at the shooting range, she paid for her gun and ammo in cash, [ill gotten no doubt], and we left. It was easy.

A few days later Mom called to tell me she'd been to the shooting range for target practice and she was still a pretty good shot. She said she'd been able to hit the man shape inside the big bulls eye in some very important places. The next time I went to her house, she had the shot up target from the range taped to her kitchen door window, facing out. Nobody ever bothered her again.

Once when she was coming to pick me up at the airport, back when you could still go through security and meet someone at their arrival gate, Mom got there early, wearing her purple overalls and leather sandals and heavy Mexican gold hoop earrings, and carrying a big brown leather purse. In the purse, she kept only three things - her keys, the gun and a five dollar bill.

Moving awkwardly out of the crowded airplane and into the arrival area with a lot of hand luggage, I looked for her but she wasn't there. A nervous looking young black porter approached and asked if I was Jessica. Yes I was, and "where's my mom?" It turned out that she couldn't enter the arrivals area with a gun, so she did the logical thing - she offered to tip the porter five dollars to hold it for her while she met me at the gate. He refused and suggested she tip him five dollars to meet me himself.

Visiting my Mom, the gun was always turning up where it was least expected. Sitting on the couch for forty five minutes watching tv...what's this lump under the cushion? Oh, it's the gun. My kids would be hanging out on her high, old fashioned four poster bed on the heavy white bedspread, petting one of several cats, and, what's this under the pillow? Mom, it's the gun!

When my amazing mother died, my mother who loved to sing, who would be forever nine years old and only wanted enough to eat and to have her own pony and for her dad to leave her alone when he was drinking; my mother who was a Grey Panther and a force to be reckoned with; my mother who became a radical socialist and got the wrongfully imprisoned out of jail, who would give you one if she had two... died at 64, in poverty, as idealists often do. She had a heart attack, driving alone in her unheated car on a cold ride to the city at Christmas time. She hung on until Dec 28th. All four of her living children and our partners met at her little house. My sister had our mother's ashes in a small cardboard box from the funeral home.

Mom's friends had given us permission to hold a little ceremony and bury the box anywhere we wanted on their land. We were greeted by two elderly bohemian ladies who said how much they had loved her. It was January and bitter cold outside but the boys managed to dig a hole under a stand of trees near the road. I sang one of her songs, "Believe Me If All Those Endearing Young Charms", and we buried the box, hugged each other, and drove back to our mother's little rented house which had to be cleared out immediately.

There were tears, and everyone seemed so young and lost, and I am the oldest, and my sister is the most organized, and my brothers were so sad and I remembered them in their high chairs a long time ago, eating peaches from the garden. One brother said, "I don't want this stuff, I want my Mom!", and I told him we couldn't have our Mom but he had to have some stuff and he had to choose it now. The other brother, who'd been searching through her clothes, held up the gun. Our mother's gun. We all told him he couldn't have it and besides we didn't have the papers for it. He took it. He wanted it. He probably got it re-registered.

IT DOESN'T TAKE LONG
TO GROW OLD

It doesn't take long to grow old
a few journeys
a few joys
suffering
and a few great parties
sirens
cook a few meals
children are born
it doesn't take long
walk a long way
worry a bit
make love to a stranger
realize all your lovers have been strangers
someone dies due to an offhand comment
bite your lip
hold back tears
and now
it doesn't take long to grow old
travel
there was a beautiful dress
a blow to the head
autumn colors
mountains fields and the sea
an entire life
and it's only a dream
there is no tomorrow
and the only things you can count on are the miracles

it doesn't take long to grow old.

STREET PRIESTESS

I live in the French Quarter
in half of a twelve room shot gun house
on Bourbon Street
where two elderly sisters lived for twenty years
without ever fixing anything
I love this house
this house loves me
I have never felt so loved by a house

in this house there are no inanimate objects
it's like the castle in Beauty and the Beast
where everything goes about it's business
and as it is in the castle of the Beast
there can be no loneliness in this house
if you are lonely in this house
it must be that you were already lonely when you arrived.

that happens to me sometimes
then I know that I must reach outside myself
to the dining table
which tells marvelous stories
who did what to whom in several languages
the salad bowl reveals the final thoughts
of cucumbers and tomatoes
with a vinegary wit
the bath is deep
the walls have ears
it is a democratic household
where everyone and everything has a say.

Living in a house where everything has a say
I become a sort of benign dictator...
my friend Richard once remarked
that in his opinion

democracy never works
being inherently unstable.
Richard felt that the best form of social organization
must be a benign dictatorship.
He himself was very democratic, never worked
and was inherently unstable
so perhaps he knew what he was talking about.

In the early evening
we sit on the front stoop
drinking wine on Bourbon Street
my dog is there
her name is Rania Dzukel
she is part coyote on my side of the family
she is beautiful and intelligent and uncombed
she is young and wears a rhinestone collar
her fur is golden
her trousers are curly

holding her leash we play tactile telephone
down the cord connecting my hand to her throat
there is love
there is regard
there are minor attempts at deception on either end.
Rania enjoys the social life of the stoop
she has become more calm with strangers
who reach out to touch her as they pass by
this makes a mockery of her position as Watchdog
but puts her squarely in the fray
of Public Relations.

I take my hair down
and drink more wine.
People from New Jersey and Paris
Houston and Tokyo
Egypt, Germany and Metarie
all the world's a stage
people from the neighborhood walk to and from work

to Matassa's or the dog park
looking for love or dinner or salvation or intoxication...

It's beginning to get dark
and Angus slips out like a shadow
to join us on the stoop.
Angus came from England
ten years ago
in a box
he is a small cat
his fur is long and black
his eyes are yellow
he is wise
I know he is wise because the part of me that is wise
observes it to be true
and surely he is at the height of his powers
in his thirteenth year.

"The tiger does not declare his tigeritude
before he pounces.
He declares it in the elegance of his leap"
Wole Soyinka, the African poet , has written.
Ah, wise.

Night has fallen
my hair is dark
my dress is loose
my wine is red
my dog is wild
my cat is black
and he is thirteen years old
I am aware and alive and never alone
in the shadows on my stoop
on the street of intoxication
I have become a nail and weigh nothing on the outside
and on the inside I weigh onehundredthousand pounds
and I hold this sweet house into the ground
keeping it right here where it's always been

since it's been at all
and I am one thousand years old
and there are no inanimate objects
oh
I am very quiet
but I am very busy.

I am not a vampire
I kiss you and your wounds heal
your blood flows thick and warm in your own veins
I kiss you
and your heart is your own
and you love the dark and you love the light
and you love your lover
and later
I light a candle.
Sometimes I kiss my food.
There are no inanimate objects in my house.

I have often sat on the street before
I have eaten and slept and got high
and made love and changed the world
on the street
spoken in tongues and frightened a palm reader
eaten watermelon
conversed with strangers who spoke no English
walked miles barefoot
carried a burden too heavy
disappeared fearful
comforted the tearful
woken up cheerful
gave the world an earful
nursed babies
begged for quarters
on the street
on many streets

once I was all one sex and telepathic
now I am a lake

a lake on a stoop
on the street of intoxication
my power has come from the street
now I spend days and nights
in the Temple of the House of the Old Sisters
street priestess
light of the love of raving lunatics
dog shit
half full go cups
lost underwear
on Bourbon Street in the morning light
the gutters really do sparkle with glitter

I cannot listen to these discarded objects any longer
too much heartache too many mind warps
I am a busy woman
I've got a whole house to talk to
and when I scry the human heart
I have to cry all your uncried tears for you
that's just one job out of hundreds
I can't do it all
cry your own damn tears and get on with your life
break your own damn heart
I'm getting older
my time is more precious
and please make love with somebody
and enjoy your food
and share your food
and share your fears
they get smaller the more people you divide them up with
unlike loaves and fishes
more like chili peppers

and as two girls approached the stoop
in the shadow and the streetlight
they stopped and made a big detour
into the road around a parked car
in front of the house

thinking they were afraid of my coyote dog
I said
"don't worry, she's a sweet dog , you can walk by here"
and I could see by their body language that these two girls
would never in their wildest moments
want to walk by my stoop
and my speaking only made it worse
because these smart girls were from New Orleans
and they knew
just by looking
that Angus was thirteen years old
a black cat at the height of his powers
and that I was a spirit made of red wine
mixed with the dust of too many streets
and the blood of my ancestors
eight nations in four generations
a spirit shaped like an invisible nail
and to walk by here might mean
having to cry their own tears
cause I quit but someone's got to do it
so
kissed and blessed
they avoided us
they avoided us
ah, wise
but too late...
for as my youthful beauty slips into the memory of this old house
and the transparency of age begins to glow around my edges
the Power
to kiss and to bless at a distance
grows stronger.

DREAM POEM

Written in My Sleep

The Moon tonight
is bound for glory,
sleeping with her boots on
and why shouldn't she

Waking in the early morning
bowing to the North, the East, the South, the West;
bowing to the Sky and the Earth -
these are her Parameters.

Then off to that other world, where
she is someone else's Moon.
In these realms they never fight
only dance to her and call her Friend

no argument there
[perhaps a quibble at the ball]
but only rolling easy
with the Moon

MY HEART HAS A LIFE OF ITS OWN

My heart:
is perfect in every way
shinier than a new one
walks on siver thumbtacks
is a beacon
always uses the good china
my heart
doesn't know how to say no
pisses standing up
still has it's wisdom teeth
keeps an altar to St Francis
is a well at night and a mountain in the daytime
keeps bees
can see in the dark
still doesn't understand.

***

STRANGE CATHEDRAL

there is a strange cathedral
underneath my ribs
softly glows
the rose window
of my heart

MAY QUESTIONS FILL THE AIR
WHERE I HAVE BEEN

Bear crow daddylonglegs and honeybee
Toad owl and red hen
tall grass tiny flowers
pinenut and lily
westward northlight
yellow skin
dry hard dusty
golden warm amber
opium ruby pearl
corn rice
hemp linen silk
a long road...
questions,comfort,touching,order;
delight in disorder:
the lovely feel of an unanswered question
lifting the air lilting
accepted questions
like spring like autumn
like a mirror in the forest
like gifts for trees
like friendship with an insect
like puppy paws...
come live with me and be my love
and we can ask questions
and leave them hanging in midair
some delicate
some too heavy to fly...
may questions fill the air
where I have been

RECKLESS

Sometimes I am reckless
sometimes I have burned too bright
be fearless in love
always be fearless in love

love is
the shining darshan moment
being - to - being
buying stamps
petting the neighbors cat
answering the phone
and sometimes the telephone that rings
in your heart
across a crowded room
I am reckless
I always answer the phone
life is short
I don't want to miss a call
I burn bright bright
to light the night night

because
I may be reckless
but I want to see any chance for love
not just 'God   bless the day I found you
I want to stay around you'...
it may be that much of the sorrow in the world exists
because in English
there is only one word for love

what I mean is the love
of when the pizza arrives
the love of taxi drivers
and plants that need to be watered twice a day

and when you only have a tiny tip for the bartender and you leave it
anyway
and dyeing Kathleen's hair blue
and potential new boyfriends
and respect respect respect
for fellow beings
who live in this same crazy world
and full of care
careful
go about their business
while I careen reckless in love
and burning too bright
through the wild ride of this incarnation

crazy - in - love fearless so bright
take a chance take a chance take a chance on me
any chance to be
fearless in love

you kiss me you bless me
near or far away
I'm a little comet
I'll be back around
good night good night good night

THE BEAUTY OF AN OLDER WOMAN

for Diana Vreeland

The beauty of an older woman
the cool assurance
of an elegant death
comforting
frightening
inevitable

The beauty of an older woman
equal parts
circumstance
artifice
and unshakeable composure

Death comes to a beautiful older woman
and, due to circumstance
can show no mercy...
he comes to her graciously,
and she is gracious;
embracing her in her elegance,
he strips it from her and leaves it
on the lawn.
They wander off

News at Ten

we have to make art
it's the only thing that will still be here
when the computer shuts down
to tell us remind us
who we were what we thought
what we did
where we were headed

when the computer shuts down
ending the i.v. flow
of news and information
entertainment
instant feedback
automatic automation
electric electrification

will the flow
slow
to become a trickle
and stop
drip drop?

or will it cease suddenly

leaving the bewildered silence

of hearts long broken
unknowing
heart pieces, mind pieces
held together by some
crazy automatic computer generated
electric glue

when the plug is pulled
we will come outside and look around

and all there will be as signposts
on that dark night
in that still day
all that will stay
doing what it always does
is art.

The most available will be advertising;
then the grafitti,murals,posters,
the crazy street singers,
the mad rehearsers,
the writers with pencils,
chalk on the sidewalk,
poets who just won't shut up,
jugglers, sword swallowers, fashion victims,
and pray-ers aloud
will be doing what they've always done:
generating their own news and information
top of the hour, every hour
what's going on?
who are we?
why are we here?
what's up, buttercup?
News at Ten

ENGLISH AS A SECOND LANGUAGE

if any of this sounds like a rough translation
please know
there are no words for these things
in any language

this is a translation
as sure as you're born
translated from unspeakable silence
into English
English as a second language

our first language must be silence
all our best work is done in silence
and our best work
may not survive translation

Jessica Ruby Radcliffe lives in New Orleans, Louisiana.

Printed in Great Britain
by Amazon